Praise for the Work of Marge Piercy:

"An immensely gifted poet and novelist. There is no denying that each of her novels has been breathtakingly ambitious and clearly the work of a major talent."
—*New York Times Book Review*

"Marge Piercy is one of our boldest and most prolific writers."
—*Los Angeles Times Book Review*

Praise for the Work of Ira Wood:

"Fresh. Vital. Totally convincing. Mr. Wood has a special gift for heartwarming comedy."
—*New York Times Book Review*

"With *Going Public* Ira Wood has fashioned a wickedly delicious and very modern romance full of wit, common sense and real love."
—Alice Hoffman

Praise for their last collaboration, *Storm Tide*:

Storm Tide "speaks with one powerful voice, moving inexorably toward tragedy even as it offers a hint of redemption."
—*New York Times Book Review*

"Marge Piercy and Ira Wood know how to play with fire and deliver a confident page burner."
—*Los Angeles Times*

"A carefully, artfully and…seamlessly told story…The reader is totally engrossed."
—*Booklist*

"*Storm Tide* is a great mystery, an intelligent political thriller, and an emotional hurricane. It's also erotic to the core, and written to be read as fast as a fierce nor'easter blowing hard across the turbulent water. From first page to last I couldn't put it down."
—John Nichols

Books by Marge Piercy

POETRY

Breaking Camp
Hard Loving
4-Telling (with Emmett Jarrett, Dick Lourie, Robert Hershon)
To Be of Use
Living in the Open
The Twelve Spoked Wheel Flashing
The Moon is Always Female
Circles on the Water: Selected Poems
Stone, Paper, Knife
My Mother's Body
Available Light
Mars and Her Children
What Are Big Girls Made Of?
Early Grrrl: The Early Poems of Marge Piercy
The Art of Blessing the Day: Poems with a Jewish Theme
Storm Tide (with Ira Wood)

FICTION

Going Down Fast
Dance the Eagle to Sleep
Small Changes
Woman on the Edge of Time
The High Cost of Living
Vida
Braided Lives
Fly Away Home
Gone To Soldiers
Summer People
He, She, and It
The Longings of Women
City of Darkness, City of Light
Storm Tide (with Ira Wood)
Three Women

OTHER

Parti-Colored Blocks for a Quilt: Essays
Early Ripening: American Women's Poetry Now: An Anthology
The Earth Shines Secretly: A Book of Days

Books by Ira Wood

The Kitchen Man
Going Public
The Last White Class: A Play (with Marge Piercy)
Storm Tide (with Marge Piercy)

So You Want to
WRITE

So You Want to
WRITE

HOW TO MASTER THE CRAFT
OF WRITING FICTION
AND PERSONAL NARRATIVE

MARGE PIERCY
& IRA WOOD

PIATKUS

Copyright © 2001 Marge Piercy and Ira Wood

First published in Great Britain in 2002 by
Judy Piatkus (Publishers) Limited
5 Windmill Street
London W1T 2JA
e-mail: info@piatkus.co.uk

First published in the United States in 2001 by The Leapfrog Press

The moral right of the author has been asserted

A catalogue record for this book is available from the British Library

ISBN 0 7499 2387 3

Text design by Paul Saunders

This book has been printed on paper manufactured with respect for the
environment using wood from managed sustainable resources

Printed and bound in Great Britain by MPG Books, Bodmin, Cornwall

*For the Young Who Want To**

Talent is what they say
you have after the novel
is published and favorably
reviewed. Beforehand what
you have is a tedious
delusion, a hobby like knitting.

Work is what you have done
after the play is produced
and the audience claps.
Before that friends keep asking
When you are planning to go
out and get a job.

Genius is what they know you
had after the third volume
of remarkable poems. Earlier
they accuse you of withdrawing,
ask why you don't have a baby,
call you a bum.

The reason people want M.F.A.'s,
take workshops with fancy names
when all you can really
learn is a few techniques,
typing instructions and somebody else's mannerisms

is that every artist lacks
a license to hang on the wall
like your optician, your vet
proving you may be a clumsy sadist
whose fillings fall into the stew
but you're certified a dentist.

The real writer is one
who really writes. Talent
is an invention like phlogiston
after the fact of fire.
Work is its own cure. You have to
like it better than being loved.

*From *Circles on the Water: Selected Poems of Marge Piercy,* published by Alfred A. Knopf, NY 1982. © 1982 by Marge Piercy

Contents

Introduction   1

1. Sharpening Your Innate Skills   4

2. Beginnings   13

3. Characterization   30

4. The Uses of Dialogue   53

5. Plot in the Novel   65

6. Personal Narrative Strategies   85

7. Choosing and Manipulating Viewpoint   95

8. Descriptions   105

9. When You Have Research to Do   115

10. A Scandal in the Family   121

11. Work and Other Habits   129

12. Practical Information for You   140

13. Frequently Answered Questions   151

Appendix I   159

Appendix II   170

Resources   176

Index   178

A Note About the Authors   181

Acknowledgments of Excerpts   182

Introduction

THIS BOOK IS A PRODUCT of workshops we have given for many years. We usually teach personal narrative or fiction together, but each of us has also taught a version of both courses alone. The "I" throughout the manuscript is one or the other of us; we felt it did not really matter which, and was less awkward than the royal "we" when speaking of something one of us wrote or did. In actual team-taught workshops, we divide up the topics, but we have each worked on every essay in this book.

In workshops, we use examples from many writers – but the problem of paying for permissions has led us to use only our own work or that of writers published by our press, Leapfrog. It is not egotism but the desire to keep the price of this book down that has led us to quote so freely from ourselves.

You will find that throughout the book we will refer you to many memoirs and novels. We do this in the earnest hope that you will not only read, for example, the beginning of a piece cited as having a good one but go on reading. Since we've begun teaching these master classes together, we've noticed an alarming trend. Students ask us what to read to improve their writing and seem disappointed when we do not refer them to the hundreds of books that have appeared on the market in the last decade that are "about" writing, or "the process" of writing, or the "path" or the "journey" taken by writers. Reading itself – the habit of reading, the immersion in books, learning how other writers have solved the same problems – seems to students less important than developing the perfect attitude toward writing or fitting writing into a life the way they might schedule time at the gym. Great writing has been done in prisons and cramped hotel rooms and commuter trains, on rickety tables in noisy restaurants, at four in the morning before the twelve-hour work day begins. Such writing has been done by people who experienced the need to write as strongly as they experienced thirst. People seem to take it as a given that great movies have been made by those who have immersed themselves in the cinema, who find true passion on a screen in a room with no windows. Yet these same people bridle when we tell them that to be a good writer you should be as well versed in literature as Martin Scorcese is in the films of John Ford. You would not want to be defended in court by a lawyer who had read only *The Attorney's Journey* and neglected to study case law. Likewise it seems absurd that people who want to write memoirs don't think it necessary to read the memoirs others have written before them.

Of course if you are not writing primarily to be published and read, you may not need or wish to be informed of the state of your art. The choice to write in journals for therapeutic reasons and for self-expression is a righteous one. Some journals, after intensive editing, have been published and beloved. Often these have been the works of experienced writers or people who have lived through extraordinary times. Such memoirs have been more carefully shaped than the word journal might imply.

Nevertheless, this book is about writing to be published; about learning the elements of craft that modern readers have come to expect, such as the ability to seduce your reader with a good beginning and to create characters who are more than stereotypes. Most writers use notebooks in one way or another, whether in the form of a laptop or a spiral pad or even scraps of paper napkins: some way of capturing random ideas or snippets of dialogue overheard or insights from a nightmare. This note-taking is not to be confused with the journal kept by a young man in one of our classes who had over a thousand single-spaced handwritten pages about his family that he expected us to tell him how to turn into a novel. For well over a year he had been dutifully writing down his thoughts when he woke up every morning. Now he was overwhelmed by the task of recopying and editing these impressions and memories into a manuscript with a shape: a beginning, a plot, and characters who could come to life in a mind other than his own. (For instance, a father who had needs and motivations and a history understandable to a reader, as opposed to the workaholic bully who was all the writer saw when imagining his dad.) Eventually, he decided to start from scratch on the novel and use his journal as a reference.

Where we have included exercises, we recommend actually trying them, to get full benefit. We ask people to do these in our classes and have found they work. A number of people who have taken our workshops have gone on to publish, some quite successfully; many make the leap to actually submitting their work to book publishers and magazines, while others have used these essays and exercises to motivate their own students. We don't for a moment imagine that our advice is the best you can find. It is simply the distillation of many years (forty-five for Marge; twenty-five for Ira) of writing experience. What we most hope to communicate, in our classes and in this book, are the skills necessary to read critically. That is, what to look for as you read, what questions to ask. How have other writers solved the problems of drawing in a reader who is faced with thousands of other titles? How have other writers used dialogue to advance their plot?

We have a dear friend who hates cookbooks. Whenever she makes a casserole or creates a soup, she insists on inventing from scratch. She thinks it's more creative, or that she's avoiding the reenactment of her mother's tired life. The product leaves much to be desired. Roast lamb really isn't very good well done in salsa. Cashews are seldom found in tomato soup for a reason. We hope you won't write like this dear woman cooks. You don't have to reinvent the wheel or the novel. There is always room for innovation, but you won't know what's new and what's tired if you don't read widely and critically. This book is a craft workshop on paper, but if you only read it without trying out at least some of what is suggested, you won't get the maximum benefit.

1

Sharpening
Your Innate Skills

BELIEVE THE BARRIERS to creativity are both inner and outer. The distinction between madness and sanity is one made by those around us: they honor us or they commit us. An act that brings admiration in one society will get you locked up in another. Seeing visions was a prerequisite for adulthood in plains Indian societies, and quite dangerous today. Societies also differ in how they regard the artist, how integrated into the ordinary work of the community she or he is regarded as being, how nearly the society regards artistic production as real production, as a reasonable adult activity, a job, in other words.

Working in any of the arts in this society is a self-elected activity. Although parents may force music lessons on their children, I have never heard of a parent who did not try to discourage a child who decided to become a composer. Even the occasional bit of back-slapping advice you get from peers is usually based on the misapprehension that writing is much easier than it is and that it is infinitely better paid than is the case. If you tell a friend one week that you are trying to start a novel, likely they will ask you what you are doing the next month, be astonished that you are still writing the same novel, and so on; and when you have finished, they will ask if you have sold it yet, as if selling a novel were easy.

Basically there is little support in our culture for apprenticeship. Even in a relatively adult movie such as *Amadeus*, the proof of Mozart's genius is that he doesn't correct, doesn't hesitate, but the music gushes out of him almost too fast for him to write it down.

In writing there is always more to read, study, learn, try out, master. The more you as a writer are open to understanding the your country and the world we live in as richly and variously cultured, the more there is to learn, the more different strands of language and crafts you will apprentice yourself to. It is not nearly sufficient to know and know thoroughly British and American literature, even if you throw in, as we increasingly must, Canadian and Australian authors. Who would strive to understand contemporary literature without Atwood, Munro, Keneally, White? But lacking a knowledge of Japanese literature, of French, of Italian, of Spanish, of South American and Mexican literature, of Russian, of Scandinavian, of Greek, of contemporary African writing, all makes us stupider than we can afford to be if we mean to write. Most foreign literatures you will read in translation, although being in command of at least one foreign language helps a writer immensely in understanding her own.

If you want to write a memoir, read memoirs. If you want to write science fiction, read science fiction. Often in workshops, participants will ask us to recommend a "how to write" book – like this one. But the truth of the matter is, the best books you can read on how to write are books that are in the genre you want to write in. What we hope to teach you, in part, is to read like a writer: to read noticing craft. The books you don't think work well may teach you as much as the ones that wring admiration from you. Whatever the author is doing, you want to ask how and look at the choices made.

All of this notion of apprenticeship is at odds with the model of success in the arts so many young people bring to bear, mostly from the careers of rock musicians. You can make it as a rock musician with three or four chords and a gimmick, at least for one record; but you can also be a has-been at twenty-two. There are equivalents among writers, but not many. Basically you may publish an occasional poem or short story in college, usually in the college literary magazine, but few serious writers reach visibility before thirty to thirty-five.

Giant conglomerates control the big media and own the publishing houses. They are run the same as other large conglomerates and would like to put out generic products like brands of toothpaste or breakfast cereal with an assured cut of a guaranteed market. Books, real books, are risky. Better financial projections can be obtained on the *All Chocolate Eat Yourself Skinny Diet Book*, thrillers that like the movies *Halloween 14* and *Die Hard 56* offer exactly the same product in a slightly jazzier package, the romance, the success story. It no longer shocks people to hear that chain and the large on-line booksellers rent space to publishers the same way that supermarkets sell the most ideal shelves for corn chips and pretzels. Publishers can pay to have their titles stacked at the front table, or positioned face-out at the check out counter and at the ends of aisles. Large publishers, of course, can better afford the many thousands of dollars it may cost for a themed twelve-copy display or a large window sign. But they expect a return on their investment and the best chance of getting that return is with a product that got one before. It's not some evil plan, just a business plan. But these criteria work against all writers who want to do original work.

The inner and outer barriers interact, because we tend to internalize rejection and lack of recognition, and because of our programming by the media and our peers.

Work in the arts requires your best energy. That means figuring out how in the course of a life that usually includes another full-time job whether paid or unpaid, you can organize your time so that you write with your best energy, not your slackest. That may require getting up before everyone else in your house or your close circle is up; it may mean working after everyone else is in bed. It certainly means having time that is devoted to work, when you pull the phone out of its jack and do not answer the door. If you have children and thus cannot quite cut yourself off from interruption, you can attempt to make it clear that only an emergency is suitable for interrupting you. You may feel guilty setting boundaries, but what kind of adults will grow from never learning that other people have boundaries that must not be crossed? Should they not rather learn what I hope you have realized, that work is precious and concentration is to be valued, to be sharpened, to be refined? We will look more carefully at organizing time when we take up work habits.

What I will return to again and again is the ability to use your mind mindfully and purposefully. To know when to go with the flow and when to turn on the cold critical eye. To know when to loose your imagination and when to keep it under control. Concentration is learned by practicing it, just as is any other form of exercise or excellence. Even when what is being concentrated on is something in the past of the writer or some nuance of feeling or precise tremor of the emotions, the writer at work is not the emotion. Work has its own exhilaration. You can be happy as a clam – precisely, because not self regarding at all, but doing your own tidal work – when you are writing a poem about how somebody was cruel and nasty to you. You can even have fun writing a story imagining your own suicide. You can experience joy writing a story about total nuclear destruction, because in that clear high place where concentration is fully engaged, there is no feeling of self. Learning to reach that state and prolong it is another apprenticeship we all undergo. You have to find the work more interesting than you find yourself, even if the work is created out of your own guts and what you are writing about is your own life.

In the ancient and very modern approach to spiritual energy and experience, the Kabbalah, which is my discipline, we speak of developing the adult mind. For a writer that is particularly important. The adult mind can decide not to fuss like a adolescent because our work and our persons have experienced rejection. The adult mind can put victories or defeats into perspective. The adult mind can choose not to allow interference from the worries of the day, not to give way to irrelevant fantasies when trying to craft a meaningful fantasy. The adult mind has learned to focus and to retain focus for much longer. We can all have bad days and we can all be distracted: it is a matter of degree and how often we can combat our idiotic and self-regarding tendencies.

Beside my computer is a window and on the ledge of the window are twelve rocks. They have accumulated over the years. Each represents some place I found sacred or meaningful. When I need to focus and center my mind, I pick up the rocks and weigh them in my hands. Eventually I will settle upon a particular rock to contemplate: maybe the rock I picked up after I climbed the Acrocorinth in 1964 from the ruins of the temple of Afrodite there. Maybe one from the Oregon coast from a dawn when I experienced a strong vision. It does not really matter which stone I select. What matters is that to me these are meaningful and radiant objects that I can focus on to get rid of clutter and distraction. It is a matter of closing down the noise of the ego, of worry, of casual boredom, of gossip, of concern with what people may think, thoughts of who has not been sufficiently appreciative of my great virtues lately. It does not matter what particular pattern you use to bring yourself into sharp focus on what you are about to write. It is only necessary that you do so. For some people, their screen saver works in the same way – or a piece of meditative music. Whatever works for you, use it.

Now as a writer, one of the things which you learn to mine at will, to call up and to relinquish is memory. Again it is a case of being able to focus on the present when that is required and appropriate, but also being able to focus on a particular area of the past when you need that.

One of the resources of the poet, the novelist and the memoir writer alike is memory. Vladimir Nabokov called his memoir *Speak, Memory*; in Greek mythology, memory is the mother of the muses. You may say you have a good memory or a bad one. An eidetic memory I believe is inborn, but you can improve your memory as you can improve your tennis game or your aim.

By practicing, you can recover pieces of your childhood that you were not aware you remembered at all. There are also false memories that are interesting to explore. We all remember scenes from our childhood that we never witnessed. I have distinct memories from before my birth. These came from hearing stories as a child and imagining them so vividly that they became my own experience. You can learn to have a vivid memory again. There are books and books on improving your memory, but what they are usually dealing with is the problem of remembering the name of the insurance salesman you just met or recalling words. We all know simple mnemonics. Before I go on a trip, I always have last minute chores I must remember to do in the morning. I invent an acronym for them. Let's say COLACU. Feed CATS; OPEN hotbed; take LUNCH; turn on ANSWER- ING MACHINE; make thermos of COFFEE to go; UNPLUG computer.

But the memory I am talking about is sensual memory; it is memory that comes like Proust's, unbidden from a crumb of cake. It is memory that can be taught to come through patience and concentration. You can use what you do remember to move into what you have forgotten, by concentrating and extending your stroll through old rooms and old gardens and along half forgotten streets. Some of what you will remember you know is not so. I have memories from early childhood of enormous buildings that were not there. They only seemed enormous to me because I was so little standing looking up at them.

To a fiction writer or a poet, it does not much matter whether a memory is a true one – to the extent that any memory is "true" since five people's memories of the same event are five different and quite distinct and often contradictory memories – or a fused memory or invented memory. If it has resonance, emotive content, meaning, then it is a useful memory to possess. Memories also change, of course. If we have grown angry with a friend, the past changes. What may once have seemed a wry sense of humor is now revealed, in light of our changed perspective, to be the mean and sarcastic streak they've always used to cut us down. We have become disillusioned and what appeared before as obvious virtues and good will are shadowed in retrospect. So we rewrite big and little history as we go.

Indeed, if you are writing a memoir of your childhood and you talk with your siblings, you may find that every child grew up in a different family because each experienced that family at a different stage: the parents were older or younger, more or less affluent, getting on with each other well or badly; suffering from problems or having solved them. The world of the family is very different for the first born, the middle child, the youngest.

An Exercise in Sensual Memory

This is a simple exercise I have been using with writing workshops for twenty years. Sometimes, I use it myself. It's almost a mediation, so it is best attempted in a comfortable position, whatever that may be for you, and in a quiet place, where you are not likely to be interrupted.

I will ask you to return to some particular place that was important to you in your childhood. I suggest returning to between four and eight years old, but it's your choice. In your imagination, walk down the block or the road leading to where you lived at that age, remembering you are small. If you pass a privet hedge, you do not look down into it, but you look sideways into its green density. When you come to the door, you may have to reach upward for the knob or buzzer. The door may be heavy for you and require effort to open.

I want you to enter the house or cabin or apartment you lived in at that time. I want you to pass through to a place that held some emotional resonance, some emotional importance for you at that time. Perhaps you were happy there; perhaps you felt safe; perhaps you were frightened there; perhaps you felt conflicted or uneasy. I want you to enter that room or place and experience it fully. Look at everything carefully, remembering your size and the angle from which you see the furniture. The underside of a table may be as important as the bearing surface to a young child. I want you to look at the ceiling; at the walls; at the floor. What covers the floor? I want you to touch everything. How does it feel? Is it rough, smooth, tacky, damp? I want you to use your sense of smell. Do you smell cooking odors, flowers from outside the open window, mustiness, your father's or mother's cigarette smoke, perfume, disinfectant? What do you hear? Are there windows and are they open or shut? Do you hear voices through the walls, the ceiling? Are the voices talking, singing, arguing? I want you to spend a period of time going over every inch of the room or place (I say "place" since perhaps it might be a basement, an attic, a root cellar, a garage, a hallway) and recall in full sensual detail as much as you can. Then I suggest you write down what you remember, trying to give not only the details but a sense of their resonance for you. Be extremely concrete and explicit.

I learned to do this when I was just starting out as a novelist. Recently when I wrote a full-length memoir, I did a great deal of it in order to recover pieces of my childhood I had forgotten, and to render more vivid the parts I did recall.

Writing a memoir, of course, is the intersection of memory, intent and language. Both fiction and memoir are built out of words. You use words every day to order lunch, to answer the telephone, to greet and discuss, indicating friendliness (or the lack of it if you are shrugging off unwanted attentions), passing time, exchanging information, giving advice or asking for sympathy. But when you write, you are using language in an even more purposeful way. Language is the stuff of your craft as oil paint and canvas might be that of an artist. You make out of words portraits, actions, everything that does and doesn't happen on the page and therefore in the mind of the reader. Yes, we all use language, but casually, often sloppily. Writing fiction or a memoir is not the same as writing a memo, a letter, a journal entry or an essay question.

You must become aware of the attributes of your medium, language. Language is a shaping of the air, the breath, into sounds and silences, in order to convey meaning and, often, to convey emotion. The nature of those sounds and the lengths of those silences can be used to create effects that further the intent of the writing.

Language contains in it attitude. Slender and skinny, svelte and bony are all used to describe a person of the same weight. You meet a dedicated seer. I meet a fanatic. Or the familiar conjugation of the verb: I am firm, you are stubborn, he is a pig-headed mule. I have a strong sense of justice and the courage to speak up; you are an irritable zealot who flares up at nothing. Attitude is built into language. Scientific language attempts to be neutral, but as physics tells us, we change what we observe. The history of science, as Stephen Jay Gould has so frequently described to us, is the history of attitude. What we perceive is colored by our culture, shaped by it. In the chapter on description, we will return to the practical application of those attributes of language.

As Gershom Sholem wrote about the Kabbalah long ago, much in the mystical experience is constant across culture but the forms it takes are culturally determined. Jews are more apt to hear voices uttering prophecy or see words than Christians, who usually see images. A Buddhist will not see the Virgin Mary; a Catholic mystic will not be vouchsafed a vision of Krishna or the Great Grandmother of Us All. We are all imbedded and imbued, dyed through and through with our culture.

Trying to get rid of attitude and culture merely impoverishes you. One human being isolated and alone is not a human being. We are social animals and we are artifacts of our culture. Being aware is not the same as trying to be without. We can become aware of our attitudes and our prejudices and our predispositions and choose which of them to foster and which of them to fight. But in other cultures, we are always a bit like tourists, going to the great cultural flea market and buying a great necklace or a headdress or a musical instrument to play with. Until you have lived for a time in a foreign culture, immersed in its daily life, you have no idea at all how much your country defines you.

In writing, much of this becomes important not in first draft, the early stages of creation, but in the critical stage of that process. After we have honed and practiced our concentration to the max and produced something, then we must break that oneness. We must step back mentally or even physically, by putting the work aside for a time, and then exercising the cold critical eye on it that says, of what I intended, what have I actually wrought? Maybe all, in two per cent of cases. Maybe twenty per cent of what I imagined is on paper. Maybe fifty per cent. That is the time for putting in and taking out; for altering and stretching and chopping; for rethinking choices that may have been the wrong ones for that particular work. It is time for making conscious choices about form that may have been made instinctively in first draft, rightly or wrongly. One thing that workshops and books like this one can teach is a set of questions to ask of the work after the first draft, when it is not what we want it to be. What can we do now to make the thing come out right?

In fiction, did we choose the right viewpoint character for our story? Do we need more than one viewpoint? What do we gain and lose if we shift viewpoints? Did I start my short story or novel in the correct place in the chronology of the story? Does my memoir have a compelling beginning or am I doing too much explaining before I get going? Do I need all those flashbacks that interrupt the narrative flow? How's my pacing? Is my dialogue working for characterization, local color, flavor and moving the plot along? Are my characters motivated and believable? Have I telegraphed my punches? Am I making full use of my minor characters? Do I have too many? Too few? What are the functions of each of them? Do I understand my protagonist or protagonists from the inside? Can I feel them? Have I brought them alive? Am I putting stuff into my memoir just because it happened, not because it is germane to the flow of the narrative I am crafting? It is good to remember as much as you can, but once you have remembered, you have to decide which of those memories are relevant and which are not relevant to the particular work you are engaged in. Not everything you remember matters to your story. Most of it doesn't.

We are trying to suggest to you questions to ask yourself and your work when you are not yet doing what you mean to do in a piece. In short, most of what we teach is how to start and how to revise: how to get from the rough stuff on the page to something that resembles the glorious thing in your mind's eye. The rest is how to work and keep working, and what to do with your product.

2

Beginnings

FICTION IS AS OLD A HABIT of our species as poetry. It goes back to telling a tale, the first perceptions of pattern, and narrative is still about pattern in human life. At core, it answers the question, what then? And then and then and then. And memoir is equally old: it's telling about your life, perhaps originally to children or a prospective mate or a new acquaintance.

Poetry is an art of time, as music is. Rhythms are measured against time: they are measures of time. A poem goes forward a beat at a time as a dance does, step by step, phrase by phrase. Narrative, whether fiction or memoir, is *about* time. First this, then that. Or this – then before it was that. Therefore this. From the perception of the seasons, of winter, spring, summer, fall, of the seasons of our lives, of the things that return and the things that do not return, what we seek and what we find or fail to find, and the dangers and temptations we encountered in route: these are the sources of the fictional intelligence. If you make such a choice (being kind to an old woman on the road, running down an old man, marrying Bluebeard against all advice, apprenticing yourself to a witch), what follows?

Why do ordinary people read fiction or memoirs? The most primitive answer is the most real: to get to the next page. To find out what happens next and then what happens after that; to find out how it all comes out.

That desire for finding a pattern in events – for not all happenings will satisfy us, not nearly, only the "right" ending, the proper disaster or the proper suspension or the proper reward – still functions as a major hunger we bring to the novel. We want stories that help us make sense out of our lives. We want to see all this mess mean something, even if what we discover is a shape perhaps beautiful but not necessarily comforting. Similarly, we don't want a life like a diary: I went to the store and on the way back I met my old friend George and we talked about the Red Sox and then I ate a banana. Shapelessness loses readers.

Again, the novel is about time and patterns in time. It is not a simultaneous art but one of transition and sequence. You can do a lot with juxtaposition, cutting, transitions, or the lack of them. The effect of simultaneity can be created but only by illusion. A novel or a memoir takes time to read. Therefore, the art of the novel and the art of the memoir involve much persuasion. You must convince the reader to start reading and continue reading. You must persuade her not to put the book down on page one or page one hundred. Not to skip. Fiction and memoir and indeed any kind of narrative requires constant persuasion. The uses of suspense and one of the uses of identification with characters are to make the reader go on turning pages.

You can spend six hundred pages on one night or pass over a hundred years in a sentence. You can start in the classic epic manner *in medias res*. You can start at the beginning: Josephine was born on a wild wintry night just as the old cow died. You can begin at the end: Josephine was buried on a wild wintry day just as a calf was born to the old brown cow. You can start at the end and go back to the beginning. You can start anywhere on the continuum of days and years and proceed in either direction. You can go in one large or several smaller circles. You can overlap blocks of time from different viewpoints. You can move into parallel or alternate universes. But time is always your servant and master and substance.

Our urge to read memoirs and autobiographies stems from the same source: the desire to understand a life. We believe that by looking at the lives of other people, we can better comprehend our own, both the choices that may or may not be open to us, and the values that have informed someone's life.

The motive to write about one's own life may stem from a desire to understand that life, to make sense out of it – in other words, to find a pattern in those events. Or it may stem from a desire to explain oneself, justify, apologize, demand justice. Or from a desire to teach: do as I did, and here is how I did it. Or, almost as frequently, here is how I went wrong, and don't you do likewise. Or an account of the descent and the ascent, the victory over some obstacle whether inside (addiction) or outside (race prejudice).

The beginning is the most important part of your story or your novel, because whoever does not read the beginning will never read the rest of it. You can't take the leisure to develop slowly in the first few pages. You are competing with the media and everything else going on plus all the other stories and pieces in that issue or books on that shelf for the reader's attention. Plus long before that point, if you haven't got an editor to read your manuscript, you never got published to begin with. Basically you can count on an editor reading your first page in a short story, maybe the first two pages; in a novel, you can count on the first ten pages. If you haven't grabbed them then, you're sunk. I am not saying, get your sex and violence up front. That is what a lot of writers do, but in fact it turns off as many people as it turns on, and too much of either right there may draw your pornographic voyeur but get rid of the rest of your potential audience.

However, here is the beginning of a novel by a young writer, about a young woman who uses her sexuality to control and keep men at bay:

From *Look At Me* by Lauren Porosoff Mitchell:

I brought another one home tonight. This one had a small birthmark behind his left earlobe and cool skin that smelled of coconut milk and lemon leaves. I catalogue them this way, by the most minor of their physical details, because otherwise they are not prone to distinction. The drink is always the same; though the color varies from pink to clear to amber, its effects are consistent. It convinces him that he is the one luring me away from the bar to a more private place – my bedroom, with the bare walls and white bed, antiseptic as a hospital and well-trafficked as Union Station. But private, yes. The walls of my apartment are insulated, so when I get on top and ride one of the men my neighbors don't hear. I am screaming, grunting. Sweating as my body rhythmically contracts. I rip pleasure out of them, one at a time, evening by evening. And by day I ignore the oily feel of them that does not wash off.

Sometimes I am drunk, and I awaken with a headache to find one of them asleep in my bed, his hair daubed in sweaty clumps to his face. Then

> I rise from my bed and sit at my laptop in the next room, typing in the dark until the sky bleeds vermilion. It is this light or the clicking keys that wake him; I do not know which. He sees me like that, writing in the morning light, spread out naked with one foot up on either corner of the desk, and I watch as the shame passes through his body. He goes soft. He feels he has violated me somehow, that he has transgressed some essential privacy. I observe with interest as he considers his own voyeurism, and I think every time it is silly, he probably still has the taste of me in his mouth. And yet he is afraid, inadequate, discovering me like this in the dying dark. He puts on his smoke-stinking jeans and sweat-damp polo shirt. He stumbles putting on his expensive sneakers that were flung in the entryway the night before. All the time I watch him. I don't stop watching until he half-kisses me and leaves and shuts the door softly behind him. Only then do I delete the page of Os and Js and ampersands and percent symbols, make pancakes, and start my work.

Here the sex is relevant to the theme of the novel and elicits a curiosity about this woman, who seems to have more on her mind than pleasure.

It is the curiosity of your potential editor and all your other readers that you must arouse. You may use your style to draw them in, you may use a skillful and compelling scene. Description works sometimes, but it had better be rather unusual description. I can think of a Tanith Lee novel about werewolves, *Lycanthia,* that begins with the description of a traveler arriving at a deserted train station deep in the wilderness during the winter. Although it is description, it is laden with evocative words that suggest something rather dreadful is about to happen, or perhaps has happened.

From *Storm Tide*:

> When the winter was over and my nightmares had passed, when someone else's mistakes had become the subject of local gossip, I set out for the island. I made my way in increments, although the town was all of eighteen miles square. To the bluff overlooking the tidal flats. Down the broken black road to the water's edge. To the bridge where her car was found, overturned like a turtle and buried in mud.
>
> The color of bleached bones, the shape of a crooked spine, the Squeer Island bridge was a product of willful neglect. Every ten years some town official proposed a new bridge and promptly fell into a hole full of

lawyers. The beaches were private, the summer people moneyed, the year-rounders reclusive. No one wanted the sandy ways paved or the hedgerows cut back. Your deed bought more than seclusion on Squeer Island; here life as you knew it ceased to exist.

There had been a family named Squeer, but only Stumpy was left. If you asked how the island got its name, people would say, "'Cause it's queer over there," and they didn't mean homosexual. They meant queer things happened. Peculiar things, Uncommon for a small town.

During high tide there was no access by land. The road to town flooded. Ducks paddled over the bridge. Fish darted through the guardrails. The summer people stocked their shelves with vodka and paperbacks and waited uneasily for the tide to recede. The residents lived for its return.

I left my car on the island side of the bridge. I slogged along the mud banks of the creek, driving fiddler crabs in front of me like herds of frightened crustacean sheep. The grasses were four feet high at the edge of the bank, an inch wide, sharp as razors. They mentioned lacerations across the palms; one in her right eyeball. I closed one eye. I wondered what it was like to sink in this bottomless liquid clay, this mud the fishermen called black mayonnaise. What did it feel like to die this way? They said her hair was encrusted with seaweed and crabs, that an eel had eaten into the armpit. They say she must have struggled to free herself, that as she grabbed at the grass her efforts only increased the suction of the mud. They still call it an accidental death.

What you're trying to do is get something lively or intriguing or mysterious or fascinating or peculiar moving and moving fast. Then you can go back and insert your necessary backgrounding and context. No one needs to know the name of the dead woman in the excerpt above, or why she died, or what kinds of weird things happened on the island. At this point you're competing for the reader's attention. You're hoping those questions will occur to the reader and they'll want to read on. The day has long passed when you could count on the patience required to sit through the first scene of a play (as Ibsen often did) in which the following transpires:

Maid – So the Master comes home today, Mr. Ives. And here we are knocking ourselves out to put the house to order.

Butler – It's been ten years to the day since the Master rode off, Lucy, and all we've heard has been those nasty rumors of duels and wild doings in Paris where he has been studying.

Maid – And he hasn't once written to his sweet mother, who took to her bed on the day he rode off and hasn't been downstairs since. What do you think has happened between them, Mr. Ives? Some say they had a quarrel about that young Bates girl he wanted to marry, Sally, who killed herself by jumping over a cliff not three months after he left.

Butler – Aye, and it's been ten years to the day since any of the Bates spoke to any of our family, the Livingstones, although previously they had been the best of friends ever since the two grandfathers settled here together after coming home from the Napoleonic Wars, etcetera, etcetera.

In medias res is the Latin term for in the middle of things, and that's how Homer opened the *Iliad* and that's where you should usually start, although rules were made to be broken. Nonetheless the more things are happening – that we can follow at least mostly – the more likely we are to get dragged into the story and willing to read on. Your exposition needs to be in there, but you have to learn to do it on the wing, subtly, without stopping the story and laying out everything while the characters shuffle their feet and the suspense dies till the story is stuck out in the middle of nowhere like a becalmed sailboat. You have to pass along the exposition with the story, with the characters, as you go. The trick, of course, is not to confuse the reader; she has to be able to follow it all. (We got a submission recently in which the novelist begins at an intriguing wedding; a very good place to introduce families and their conflicts. But there were too many people not sufficiently differentiated and ultimately it was confusing. It felt very much like being at a wedding and not knowing the bride's family from the groom's or whose friends were whose. Focusing more deeply on fewer characters and their conflicts might have been a better strategy.)

For instance if you are writing science fiction or speculative fiction, you must indicate some unusual things in the beginning, but not by getting lost in the hardware. You want to let the reader know right away that this is perhaps another time, another place, another planet, an alternate reality, but it is more important to introduce your characters and get your plot under way. It is more essential for the reader to be engaged and interested in what is going on and the people to whom it is happening, than that the reader grasp every detail of the situation you have created. That you have to do on the fly, in bits and pieces as the story moves on.

From *He, She and It*:

Josh, Shira's ex-husband, sat immediately in front of her in the Hall of Domestic Justice as they faced the view screen, awaiting the verdict on the custody of Ari, their son. A bead of sweat slid down the furrow of his spine – he wore a backless business suit, white for the formality of the occasion, very like her own – and it was hard even now to keep from delicately brushing his back with her scarf to dry it. The Yakamura-Stichen dome in the Nebraska desert was conditioned, of course, or they would all be dead, but it was winter now and the temperature was allowed to rise naturally to thirty Celsius in the afternoon as the sun heated the immense dome enclosing the corporate enclave. Her hands were sweating too, but from nervousness. She had grown up in a natural place and retained the ability to endure more heat than most Y-S gruds. She kept telling herself she had nothing to fear, but her stomach was clenched hard and she caught herself licking her lips again and again. Every time she called up time on her internal clock and read it in the corner of her cornea, it was at most a minute later than when last she had evoked it.

There is certainly a lot to be explained in the above excerpt. Backless business suits? A clock on the corner of her cornea? The Yakamura-Stichen dome? But it's the familiar situation in the midst of all this weirdness, the custody battle, that grounds the reader and compels attention, that causes the reader to be engaged and interested in what is going on and identify with the people to whom it is happening.

Similarly, if you are writing historical fiction, you want to give a flavor of the time and place you are writing about, but it is the characters and the situation that take precedence, not what kind of clothes they wore or the type of sailing vessels then current.

From *Gone to Soldiers*

Louise Kahan, aka Annette Hollander Sinclair, sorted her mail in the foyer of her apartment. An air letter from Paris, "You have something from your aunt Gloria," she called to Kay, who was curled up in her room listening to swing music, pretending to do her homework but being stickily obsessed with boys. Louise knew the symptoms but she had never learned the cure, not in her case, certainly not in her daughter's. Kay did not answer; presumably she could not hear over the thump of the radio.

Personal mail for Mrs. Louise Kahan in one pile. The family stuff, invitations. An occasional faux pas labeled Mr. and Mrs. Oscar Kahan. Where have you been for the past two years? Then the mail for Annette Hollander Sinclair in two stacks; one for business correspondence about rights, radio adaptations, a contract with Doubleday from her agent Charley for the collection of stories *Hidden from His Sight.* Speaking engagements, club visits, an interview Wednesday.

The second pile for Annette was fan mail, ninety-five percent from women. Finally a few items for plain Louise Kahan: her *Daily Worker,* reprints of a *Masses and Mainstream* article she had written on the Baltimore shipyard strike, a book on women factory workers from International Publishers for her to review, William Shirer's *Berlin Diary.*

Also in that pile were the afternoon papers. Normally she would pick them up first, but she could not bring herself to do so. Europe was occupied by the Nazis from sea to sea, an immense prison. Everywhere good people and old friends were shot against walls, tortured in basements, carted off to camps about which rumors were beginning to appear to be more than rumor.

For instance, if your story is about a doctor, you *could* use the first page to tell us how old she is and whether she went to an ivy league med school or a state school and what she chose to specialize in and whether she's a risk taker or plays it safe; or you could begin in the middle of open heart surgery and allow the reader to discover her background while seeing her in action. You could begin the story of this doctor at her birth and move forward through medical school, to the daring new type of heart implant that won her fame around the world. You could start with the bomb that killed her as she was washing up after the operation and go back to her birth and the difficult struggle to make it to college, no less med school, coming as she did from a dirt-poor Appalachian family. You could start with her first sexual encounter with her childhood sweetheart, Malcolm, in which she insisted on retaining her virginity, having watched her mother give birth to eight children before she was seventeen years old, and thereby losing Malcolm to another girl. There are as many ways to begin as there are stories, but the most important thing is that whatever beginning you choose to write works to intrigue the reader and entice them to read on.

This does not mean that you should stare at your computer and freeze up and write nothing until you discover the perfect place to start. Never be afraid to get going on something. You can rework your beginning endless times. All writers do. You don't have to have the perfect beginning to get to the middle – not at all. Several of my novels I began at what later became chapter two. In *Small Changes*, I actually began with what is now Chapter Six, which goes back in time and brings Miriam from her childhood up toward where we meet her in Chapter Three. It was only when I had written Miriam up to where she meets Beth that I went back in first draft and started Chapter One with Beth's marriage. Both of Ira's novels, *The Kitchen Man* and *Going Public* have as a second chapter what was originally, in early drafts, the first chapter.

From *The Kitchen Man*:

I am a spy at the elbow of the powerful, a fly on their wall. Ignored, I mingle, privy to the secrets they drop casually. I deliver pleasure. I loosen their tongues with champagne. And smile. And remember.

By night, I listen. By day, I write.

Naked, I begin the transformation.

The jeans of my day balled in a corner, I shimmy into black wool trousers, shark skin smooth, alive with prickly static. My starched shirt crackles as I break it from its cardboard bondage, my patent leather pumps twinkle sapphires of blue light.

Upstairs, rushing feet drub the ruby carpets, tap cadence on the marble floors. Chairs clack into place. Ice tumbles into silver buckets. Nervous voices shout last minute instructions and bitter complaints seethe, whispers in the cavernous hallways of Danish castles.

I tug cautiously at the wings of my tie. I flick stray fuzz from the pleats of my cummerbund. Snapping my onyx cufflinks into place, I inspect my nails. I catch my waistcoat as it tips, satin cool and shimmering, from its wooden hanger. Combing my thick moustache into perfect symmetry, clicking my heels, I turn to the mirror and bow. I am perfect. I am ready. I

am a soldier in the service of the appetites of the rich. A waiter at Les Neiges D'Antan.

The Snows of Yesterday. The finest restaurant north of New York City. Number one choice in the haute cuisine category of every magazine in which we advertise.

Until fifth draft, *Gone to Soldiers* began with what is now Chapter Four. The decision where to begin is extremely critical and often subject to much experimentation. There are two different versions of F. Scott Fiztgerald's novel *Tender is the Night*, as I recall, one beginning in Rosemary's viewpoint and one beginning in Dick's.

I can give you three rules which if not golden are certainly useful: Do not confuse the Beginning of the Story with the beginning of the events in the story. There is infinite regression in all stories, or they would all begin with the Big Bang when the universe started. The particular events you are shaping may start with the birth of your character, but that is not where the Story starts.

Secondly, never confuse the Beginning of the Story with how you begin to write it. In hindsight, there is usually a correct place to begin in the plot, but in your own work, begin writing where you can. Sometimes if you are having trouble entering a character, you can find a scene you can imagine yourself in, a point of commonalty, of empathy, where you can make a doorway into that character. That might be the first scene you write, even if it turns out to be in the middle or even at the end of the finished product.

Thirdly, no matter how cute or compelling or chic or gripping your beginning may be, if it does not lead to your story, be prepared to scrap it rather than distorting the entire book in the service of a good start. I knew a writer who won two awards on the strength of the first chapter to a novel, from which the novel not only did not but could not follow. But she could never abandon that chapter, because it was the strongest part of the book. It was arresting, all right, but all the fireworks were burned out by the end of it and it could not develop into the material she really had for a novel. Therefore, while the material paid off financially for a while, she never got a novel, never got more than a couple of excerpts published and never got on with her writing.

Even more to the point, if the rest of the book does not follow from the beginning, you will draw readers who will be disappointed. They thought it was blood and guts, but it's a tender psychological study of a boy who loves a pigeon; they thought it was going to be a humorous trip through contemporary adolescence, but it is a psychopath's revenge. The beginning must be powerful or inviting, but it must begin what you are actually going to continue.

If you are working with multiple viewpoints in a novel, it is worth serious consideration which character should open your book. Sometimes it is a matter of chronology; sometimes of opening with the most intriguing or inviting character. There is no reason it should be the most important, unless that's a great idea for other reasons. Since I use multiple viewpoint a great deal, I often shuffle my early chapters until I find the best arrangement. The beginning is that important: it is all important. Without a good beginning, no one with the possible exception of your mother or partner will ever bother to continue reading what you have written.

Don't be afraid to start in the middle of things. If you're telling the story of a life, you do not have to start with childhood. Yes, someone's life starts with her birth, of course; but that doesn't have to be where your story starts. Does your story begin with your birth? With your parents' births or marriage? With your graduation or meeting your life partner? Does it start with a discovery or the desire to understand something puzzling, to solve a mystery or to change your life in some way?

From *Rookie Cop*:

Sol Hurok immigrated to the United States from the village of Pogar, Russia in 1906 and made a small living for himself by producing concerts for New York City's ever growing number of labor societies. Over the years, the workers' craving for highbrow entertainment grew to such an extent that his concerts were staged in the Hippodrome, an enormous amusement hall built by P.T. Barnum. Hurok became the personal manager of the great African-American contralto Marian Anderson and arranged the first U.S. tour for the young violin sensation and son of a poor Israeli barber, Itzak Perlman. Within several generations, Hurok became known as The Impresario, importing cultural institutions such as the Comedie Francaise and the Old Vic to perform for American audiences. A more beneficial, or benign profession would be hard to imagine.

Except that the talent he imported also included the Bolshoi Ballet and the Moiseyev Dance Company and there were those who wished to disrupt the ties between the United States and the then-Soviet Union – by any means necessary.

Hurok had been warned many times that he was to stop bringing in Soviet performers. Bottles of ammonia had been uncorked during a number of his events as well as during shows produced by Columbia Artists, a rival company that also imported Russian talent. Live mice and stink bombs had been used to cause upset to the audiences. Some performances had been disrupted by shouting. Annoying as those actions might have been, they hadn't proven effective enough. It was thought that perhaps smoke bombs, delivered right to Hurok's office, as well as those of Columbia Artists, would make the point.

A young man was given some money to buy the chemicals (hypnole and an oxygenator) in order to produce the devices. Although an effective smoke bomb needed only a few ounces of the two materials when combined, he purchased a hundred pounds of the stuff, the reasoning being, if a little smoke was good, a lot of smoke would be better. Then he and another fellow made up two bombs, each weighing thirteen pounds and placed them inside two cheap attaché cases, a small fuse jutting inconspicuously outside each, ready for the match.

This memoir does not even begin with the author, the protagonist, but with the beginning of a critical situation in his undercover work. We meet him after we have a notion of what kind of situation he had been plunged into. He is using a bombing – which will lead to a death – to bring us into the story of an episode in his life. As a rookie cop in the NYPD, he was sent undercover without training to infiltrate an organization that had just come to the notice of the powers that be, the Jewish Defense League.

Some characters in fiction or some people writing their memoirs may have had a fascinating childhood that should be covered in depth. For other characters or for yourself, you may want to whip though childhood in a few pages or tell about it on the fly. In the memoir *Rookie Cop*, the author mentions his childhood very briefly well into the narrative, and only to make the point of why he chose to enter the police department. The same holds true if your novel or story is about a particular incident. You can start in the middle of World War II and go back to when your character was drafted. You can start in the middle of a safari, as Hemingway did in "The Short Sweet Life of Francis McComber," when the main character has just committed what he believes is an act of cowardice, fill in the beginning of the story through conversation and move to the end, where his wife blows his head off.

You have to decide your best way to open. Maybe it's an event, a marriage or ceremony where your main characters are all assembled. Dorothy Allison in her novel, *Bastard Out of Carolina,* puts all the important characters, the women in her family, inside a speeding car with the implication that something important is about to happen and with a strong sense of the social class and regional sense of the characters. Maybe you want to start with a moment of revelation, when everything that preceded it comes suddenly into perspective and everything afterwards is seen through an enlightened perspective. Maybe your story starts with a moment of outrageous good fortune, the birth of a child; or a moment of torment, like the death of one. Maybe it starts with a strange coincidence: seeing an old lover again after ten years or overhearing a phone call that terrifies or enlightens you.

You might start with a general statement about yourself that you hope will generate curiosity or empathy or identification in your reader. This is the opening of my memoir *Sleeping with Cats*:

Do I have faith in my memory? Who doesn't? How can I not trust memory. It is as if I were to develop a mistrust for my right hand or my left foot. Yet I am quite aware that my memory is far from perfect. I frequently forget events and people that my husband, Ira Wood, remembers, and similarly, I remember incidents that have slipped away from him. I rarely remember things incorrectly; mostly I remember clearly or I forget completely.

I have distinct memories of events that happened before I was born or for which I was not present. This comes from having heard the stories told vividly by my mother or my grandmother when I was little and imagining those scenes and the people in them so clearly and intensely that I experience them as my own. I have precise memories of the voice and face of my mother's father, who died ten years before my birth. Stories about him that I heard as a child were so real to me that I created him as a living personage.

In our experience, the best way to learn how to write good beginnings is to read what others have written and discover how they solved the same problems you will face. Don't worry about imitating what they've written because your vision, your plot, your characters will be unique to your story. Nor should you worry about liking every beginning you read. You can learn as much from writing you consider to be dreadful as you can from the pieces you admire.

There are a number of books on writing that emphasize the necessity of starting with a snappy first sentence. We are more concerned with the *situation* you choose to begin with, and the way various writers have solved the problem of attempting to hook the reader.

Gore Vidal begins his memoir *Palimpsest* with the wedding of two members of high society in "the church of the presidents" across the avenue from the White House, where he was one of the ushers, JFK was another, and Jackie Kennedy went off to the bathroom with the bride and showed her how to douche, post-sex. Name-dropping, the hint of scandal, the promise of gossip and the insider's view of the lives of the rich and famous, are Vidal's hooks.

In *The Mambo Kings Play Songs of Love*, Oscar Hijuelos attempts to seduce his readers with nostalgia, as he evokes the kind of inner city neighborhood few of us live in anymore. On LaSalle Street, in the 1950's, kids play in the courtyard as mothers doing housework watch everybody's kids, not only their own, from their windows. Mrs. Shannon, the Irish lady "in her perpetually soup-stained dress" calls out to Cesar to tell him his favorite episode of *I Love Lucy* is on, the one in which his father and uncle appeared as Cuban cousins of Desi Arnaz at the Tropicana nightclub. Most readers have heard of *I Love Lucy*; many would be intrigued by a young kid whose relatives were somehow attached to the show.

Piri Thomas starts his autobiographical collection of short stories set in prison, *Seven Long Times*, during a stick-up in a bar. He recounts the role every member of his gang had played many times before, where each man positioned himself and how they signaled each other, how they herded the customers against the wall and approached the bartender. But this time something goes hopelessly wrong. Curious?

Lillian Hellman begins her memoir *Pentimento* one foggy summer morning on Martha's Vineyard when, during an ordinary swim, she is sucked under by a riptide and almost drowns. Thinking she is about to die, she bashes her head against the pilings of a pier and imagines herself in a conversation with former lover, Dashiell Hammet, "a man who had been dead five years."

Simone de Beauvoir decides to start *Memoirs of a Dutiful Daughter* on the day she was born. Turning the pages of a picture album, describing photographs of her proper French family, she risks losing many readers who would be fascinated with her courageous and unorthodox life but bored by an ordinary bourgeois childhood until, describing her relationship to her little sister, she proves herself to be anything but an ordinary child. "I felt myself to be much more interesting than an infant bundled up in a cradle. I had a little sister; that doll-like creature didn't have me."

Cesare Casella (with Eileen Daspin) tells the story of his life in a cookbook entitled, *Diary of a Tuscan Chef.* Family experiences are intermingled with recipes in this memoir and in the first chapter he posits that he doesn't exactly know where he was conceived but if he had to guess, he'd say the kitchen, and goes on to describe, in delicious sensual detail, the room, the region and the people that so influenced his life. Anyone who hungers for "dusty rounds of pecorino put up for the winter, tins of salted anchovies to eat with bread. . . and liters upon liters of vino delle colline Lucchesi" cannot fail to read on.

William Gibson begins his cyber-punk novel *Count Zero* with his hero Turner being chased through the ghettos of India by an intelligent bomb called a Slamhound filled with "a kilogram of recrystallized hexogene and flaked TNT." What's a Slamhound exactly? Why is it chasing him? Is there such a thing as recrystallized hexogene? Who cares? Turner is blown to bits and it takes three months to put him together again, with eyes and genitals bought on the open market. It's the speed, the violence, the absurd details of the author's future world that keep the reader wondering, What the hell is going on?

There are beginnings that seduce simply by creating an identification between the readers and characters. In the short story, "Storm" Edna O'Brien begins with a mother, a son and his fiancée on summer holiday together. We are drawn into the mother's slow observation and growing jealousy of their relationship, which is making her feel old. Mary Flanagan begins her story "Cream Sauce" with Lydia, the world's slowest cook. Lydia likes to drink Bordeaux as she prepares dinner, while her suffering family is enticed by "tantalizing aromas accompanied by interminable waits" likely to be followed by "not infrequent failures which must, out of sheer physical necessity, be consumed." Anybody who cooks, or lives with a cook like Lydia, would read on.

Exercise

The decision about exactly what should be on page one of your novel or memoir is extremely critical, so don't hesitate to experiment. In our workshops, our very first assignment is to write a dynamite beginning. The catch is, it doesn't have to be the beginning of anything you plan to finish or even to write. But it has to be a beginning that is irresistible, that when each participant reads their first page (we ask the participants to write one paragraph to one page only), the other people in their group will demand to know what happens next.

When we give this assignment on the very first night of the workshop, people always groan. "An irresistible beginning? You're cruel! We can't do that!" They start to tense up, at which point Ira always tells the following story:

Some years ago, before he became a well-known essayist, a friend had received what at that time in his career was a prestigious assignment. He had been hired by a national environmental organization to write the cover copy to accompany their annual Beaches of the World calendar and was to be paid a large stipend. I was excited for him and asked every time I saw him how it was going. The first time, he said he was doing his research, walking local beaches and driving down to Connecticut and up to Maine when time allowed. The next time I asked, he said he was considering a trip to Florida, via the beaches on Cape Hatteras. A couple of weeks later, he still hadn't started the piece and when he said he was pondering a trip to the Pacific Northwest coast, I understood that under the weight of succeeding brilliantly, he had tied himself into a knot and was afraid to start.

"You just have to ask yourself one thing," I said. "Who the hell reads a calendar?"

Later, he told me he began the piece the next day and finished it soon after.

You have to remember not to take yourself too seriously. No beginning (especially something that is the beginning of nothing) is chiseled in stone. You can tear it up, rewrite it, place it in the middle of the piece, save it as something you might use later on. The trick is simply to begin. If you don't begin, you will never finish. Moreover, be real; nothing you are likely to write will become as important as the Bill of Rights or the Magna Carta or War and Peace. And even if it should become important, it wouldn't have if you did not begin. Remember, you can always change what you write, but if you don't write it, there's nothing to improve upon. So now, begin!

3

Characterization

I T IS EASIER TO TALK about some of the factors that make for
unsuccessful characters than it is to say simply and straight out what
makes characters good. You'll discover that some people will tell you
that a given character is excellent and believable and others will find the
same character uninteresting or unbelievable. That is standard and you
learn to accumulate many opinions before deciding for yourself. In
fiction as in real life we find some people charming whom others find
boring and are repelled by some people we notice, with chagrin, that
others adore. There is a personal chemistry side to the characters in
novels, which it is folly to ignore and impossible to explain. It would be
irrelevant in approaching Rodin's statue *The Thinker* to feel that you
would like to have dinner or take in a movie with him, but when we are
dealing with characters we read about, that irrational chemistry side does
matter. We have to be able to find Vronsky attractive to identify with
Anna Karenina; if we take a violent dislike to Little Red Riding Hood, we
will be rooting for the wolf, and the story will be quite, quite different.
Often, readers can only generalize when they try to tell you why a
character worked for them – because the character is funny, they might
say – and less than honest when a character displeases them – because the
character may very well remind them of someone they don't like or
something they don't like about themselves.

However, when several readers tell you that the same character is not believable or comprehensible, you are in trouble. Often in the work of apprentice and aspiring writers there are three kinds of characters that don't work.

The first is a character based upon the writer herself, but one in which her self-hatred is in charge. Often young writers set up a piece of themselves to castigate and punish and perhaps kill off as if by that means they could get rid of the parts of themselves they most detest. Indeed often writing about some aspect of your life or yourself you find traumatic or painful is a way of dealing with that pain. But self-hatred can be a besetting sin or weakness to a novelist. The desire to punish yourself vicariously distorts the work. The writer is unable to differentiate himself or herself from the character, and therefore to create a character that is multi-dimensional and interesting. We wonder why we are supposed to want to read about this person. Often such a character is both boring and unpleasant. We may desire to step on him or her after a chapter or two as we might step on a large ant, but we have no desire to enter their experiences and live them.

Now, you could respond by pointing to the work of Philip Roth, for instance, whose characters may come right out and say, not only as far back as *Portnoy's Complaint*, but in his recent works like *Sabbath's Theater*, something like, I am a crazy person, I am about to do a detestable thing, but the difference is in the tone. The character doesn't hate himself for it. Or, put another way, the character thinks it's his only choice. In fact, acting crazy is the right thing to do, the only thing he can do. He'll tell you a hundred different reasons for it, reasons that you can even identify with. Roth's Mickey Sabbath is a hostile, self-indulgent man who treats people badly and relishes weird sex, but does so in response to his terror of dying. He does it with a kind of manic energy that draws the reader along.

Look at Kafka's Gregor Samsa, or Bruce Jay Friedman's *Stern*, same schtick: they transcend self-hatred because they take it to its ridiculous limits (turning into large cockroach, a grand metaphor for how one feels treated in the world) or find themselves in situations that are pathetic (being terrified of a suburban neighbor), but that you are able to identify with. It is not that you can't write about unsympathetic characters. The problem is to give the reader something about them to like, or be fascinated by, or curious about. It can be their humorous take on the world, their very strange world view, even their voice. You're attempting to give the reader a reason to spend time with them.

The second common problem, and this is especially relevant for memoir writing, arises with characters drawn directly from life. Often they do not work, especially if you do not know, or cannot bring yourself to imagine, the person intimately enough. It is not that you cannot use someone you know to model a character on — as long as you understand you are dealing only with a piece of them. The grandmother you adore and admire is also a person in her own right. Concentrating only on the kindness you have known from her (and neglecting, for instance, her early life, or her ornery side, or the difficulties she might have with some other members of the family) will make her less interesting than a more fully imagined seventy-five-year-old woman. And the opposite situation: you can certainly write about a person who has done you wrong, as long as you are not exercising your ambivalent feelings towards them in a way that interferes with the creation of a believable character in a believable plot. Revenge is not the best motive for writing a story. It distorts, too often.

Many times you will hear a story in a workshop and criticize the behavior of a character only to be told, but that's the way it happened. Too bad. If you do not understand a character, then you will not be able to write well about that character. If someone provoked you in real life too much for you to empathize with them or to grasp their motivation, then you will not do any better with them in print. The reader will not understand either, and that's a problem.

Often, in real life, we do not know what a character means the first time we encounter such a person. It is only the third or fourth time we meet a particular constellation of characteristics, of traits, that we can understand what is true strength and true weakness. As we get older, we find out how a lot of stories turn out in real life, and that enables us to understand our characters better and to build richer ones. After we have come to understand the characters of those around us by watching them in action under stress, in good and bad times, over many years, we can build better and more convincing characters in our stories and novels.

The problem may be that you saw only one aspect of a character, and that was an aspect you disliked. Let's say, a racist teacher or a high school drug dealer who hangs out in the mall. It is not that you cannot use someone you dislike to model a character on, but if you're going to concentrate *only* on the parts you dislike, and not imagine them more fully, it's best that that character function only as a walk-on in your story. If you have malevolent or ambiguous feelings about someone, you may not be able to allow yourself to fully imagine them as a person with an interior life and motivation. If you do not intimately understand a character, that is, take the time and make the effort to imagine all their contradictions – the good in them as well as the bad; the people they treat with kindness as well as the people they hurt – then you will not be able to write well about that character. As writers we're fascinated with the ambiguity of human behavior. People act for a variety of motives; we may kill out of intense love. We may compliment someone because we dislike them intensely. A mass murderer may be very kind to his elderly parents. The reason the legend of Robin Hood has lasted for over five centuries is that he was a mugger with sympathy for the poor.

The third type of character that tends to be less than successful is the character type drawn not from knowledge, not from observation, not from musing about people you have known and your own reactions and motivations, your weird little foibles, your personal superstitions, but from other writers, or commonly, TV and movies. With each imitation, such types are farther from reality, more plastic, and a reader feels that diminution. Such characters are made of words, not from observation or insight that informs those words. What are some types? The tough guy detective. The Jewish mother. The dumb blonde secretary. The Valley girl. The stoned-out surfer dude. The pistol-toting drug dealer from the projects wearing leather and heavy gold jewelry.

It is not that we cannot work in types. Much comedy involves types, and often so does genre writing. All writing involves some use of types. But for stock characters to work, they must be entered and made to come alive.

Let's take an example. The tough guy detective. How do we make this tired old type interesting?

1. You can write a parody by *exaggerating* the type. He keeps whiskey in his desk and when he wants a drink he bites the neck off the bottle. He speaks in monosyllables only; wears his shoulder holster in the shower; keeps a gun behind every door in his house, including the refrigerator and taped under the toilet seat.

2. You keep the type but *humanize* it. He is a tough guy detective but all those years of drinking have nearly done him in, and he is a vociferous member of AA. He takes vitamin pills by the handful and is concerned with food additives. How many detectives in mysteries today love to cook?

3. *You work against the type.* In *Play It Again, Sam* you have Woody Allen trying to be Humphrey Bogart, looking ridiculous in a trench coat and fedora, coughing when he lights up a cigarette. This is a standard device of comedy also, the comedic character who longs to be a different type than he or she is: The shlemiel who wants to be Don Juan. The klutz who wants to be an athlete. The bookish librarian who dreams of being a femme fatale.

A variation would be Columbo, if you remember the show. Instead of a tight-lipped Joe Friday, you couldn't shut the guy up. He was always interested. Drove his suspects crazy with his questions. "Oh gee, Mr. Moneybags, is that how you use arsenic on your lawn to keep down the sowbugs, that's absolutely fascinating." A slob and a family man and always having a little trouble with his car, instead of zooming around on the streets in your standard car chase.

You can work farther against type altogether by having a high school girl as a vampire-slayer; or a sweet little old lady like Miss Marple as your detective. Agatha Christie, by working against type created a type in itself, the apparently delicate but very bright spinster who seems like somebody's maiden aunt till she traps the killer. A standard in today's mystery novel is the "amateur sleuth," an ordinary person drawn into a crime they must solve. Andrew Greeley's Father Blackie Ryan is a priest detective, a Bishop, no less. Barbara Neely's Blanche White is a street smart African-American domestic.

Exercise

Think of some stock character or literary stereotype and figure out how to make it new; more engaging or more sinister. Strike, in Richard Price's novel *Clockers,* is a crack dealer in the projects. Not your typical rock-tough, fast-talking, inscrutable heavy, he has a nervous stomach, and instead of sitting on a park bench sipping malt liquor, he's rarely without a bottle of Maalox. Zel, the dentist in William Goldman's *Marathon Man* adds another dimension to a profession often overlooked in literature: he's a Nazi war criminal sadist. Figure out some of your own: The Jewish Mother assassin? The pro boxer whose passion is hybridizing day lilies? The male prostitute street hustler who is a serious student of Zen?

Now of course the first thing we notice about somebody when we are approaching them from the outside is their physical appearance: size, style, coloration, race, age, what they are wearing, the way their voice sounds, the accent, the vocabulary, the sense of style.

Nonetheless, the most important thing about your characters is seldom how they look. There are characters who are incredibly real to us, and we cannot begin to say what they look like. What does K. in Kafka's *The Trial* look like? Is he tall or short, blond or dark? Who cares? One of the clichés of fiction is to have your viewpoint character look in the mirror right off so that they can tell the reader exactly what they look like. Action stops, the story stops and we get a meaningless description. You may well want the reader to know what your character looks like, but often in apprentice writing, that's all we find out. What does their size mean to them? Do they think of themselves as normal size, when you would look at them and think, What a little guy. Do they think of themselves as oversized? You might judge such a person handsome or merely passable, but how do they feel about themselves? People's self-images are often at odds with what other people observe. A woman who appears to you very attractive may think of herself as that fat kid who wore braces and had acne. Think how that might affect her behavior. Would she walk proudly into a party or enter quietly? Would she tend to stay in a bad relationship, despite everyone who observes her wondering why? When the reader observes her buying clothing for herself, is she opting for large sizes that hide her body? Will she never go to the beach when her friends ask? Your characters might be stuck back in high school popularity contests, still trying to make the team or join the ruling clique, while they are in reality astronauts or congressmen.

Similarly, we have all known people who were raised by doting parents and who truly believe themselves to be devastating and who act accordingly, no matter how the world may fail to agree. Their self-confidence and their pleasure in the mirror never falters; it is the world that is wrong. If a man fails to accord her the value she places on herself, she thinks him afraid of a strong competent woman. If a woman fails to respond to such a character's advances, she is frigid or scared of sex and can't handle a real man. If you are over forty, you know former athletes now gone to flab who still have that confidence that came from being the best at something that was widely admired, even though those glory days are long gone. So if you describe such a person as a fifty-two-year-old flabby man with a big belly, you are missing the essence of that character, who still sees himself as the basketball star, the quarterback, the ace pitcher. Remember Inspector Clouseau of the Pink Panther movies. He runs into a wall and blames the wall. "Stee-u-pid Architect! What a ridiculous place for a wall!" Writing prose allows you the freedom to wander around in your character's mind and to exploit and develop their arrogance, their fears and insecurities, their great narcissism – traits that can bring your character alive for the reader.

Each character must be given a name. That name can suggest ethnicity, can define or not define the sex of the character. The name can suggest character. We all can remember names of the characters of Charles Dickens that define a type perfectly. Ebenezer Scrooge. Uriah Heep. Tiny Tim. Madame Defarge. Harold Skimpole. Mrs. Jellyby. Wackford Squeers. Basically you must believe you have chosen the true name of your character. Sometimes you will find that after a draft, you may change the names of one of your important characters. This is because as you have come to know them, the name is no longer appropriate. When you are writing a memoir, you have a decision whether to call a particular character Charlie Browne, or just C. or whether to tell us you have changed the names to protect the privacy of the people you are dealing with. In the latter case and in all fiction, when you are inventing a name, you might as well make up one that does a little of the work of characterization. Think even of the most commonly used names in English. Each has its own flow: Michael versus Mike. The prideful, multi-syllabic "Elizabeth" versus the softer "Beth." The formal use of the name "John" versus the free-wheeling "Jack." Who uses each form of the name to call the character? What does the character prefer? How do they introduce themselves?

How do they smell? Of sweat? Of lily of the valley? Of that ghastly stuff they spray on you in department stores if you can't run fast enough? Of coal dust or wood smoke? Of sweat and sugar icing after working in the bakery?

And what is the quality of the person's voice? How do they laugh? How do they move? How do they sit and stand and walk? How much space do they occupy? Some people contract to occupy minimal space and some, who are no physically larger, expand to occupy the entire back seat of a luxury car. The difference may depend on how much space they believe they are worth; or how they react to others touching them. As a writer, that's your raw material. You can mine it.

You might have a character who would go through four hundred pages without your ever describing a single piece of clothing, and you might have another character whose wardrobe would be an important element in that characterization. Similarly there are certain characters who are evoked in our minds by some items of clothing, such as Sherlock Holmes's deerstalker hat or Robin Hood's green tunic.

When you are entering a character, you have to feel how they move. Do they move in spurts, in long fluid motions, rapidly, mechanically, carefully? Think of a dancer; think of an old lady making her way across an icy street. What is their natural speed of action and reaction?

What senses are most important to them? When they enter a room, do they respond first to sight, sound, smell, or to abstract characteristics of the space, or to the social dimension of what is in the room. Some characters will be very observant. Their heads will be full of colors, sensations; others will interpret the world in terms of sounds, rhythms. What work a person does will affect their perception of the world. A doctor will see cases, diseases; a dentist will look at people's teeth and bite; an accountant will consider someone's financial stability; a model will look at everyone else as being fit to be photographed or not. An aging stage actor will pay attention to who recognizes him and who treats him as a nonentity.

In dealing with the nonphysical characterization devices, one set are the shallow devices of tics, hobby horses, tags, obvious habits of speech, running jokes. Deep characterization methods include fears, anxiety, desires, passions, attachments to things and to people, friendships and antipathies, real beliefs. It's a good idea to combine both methods of characterization with any of your reasonably prominent characters.

The most important thing of all to know about your protagonist or any other very important character is this, What does that character want? It is what the protagonist wants and does not want that can set the plot in motion and certainly should be one of the chief mainsprings of the action. Wanting is not always positive. A character's chief passion could be to avoid pain, rather than to achieve pleasure. A character may just want to stay alive, to continue to exist. In Jack London's famous story "To Build a Fire," the primary motivation of the only character is not to freeze to death. A character may desire to escape from a prison, a relationship, a danger. When a character wants something that another character wants also, or wants to prevent the first one from having, we have the beginnings of action. *Character A* wants to leave a marriage; *Character B*, the partner, wants the marriage to continue. But as I have tried to suggest, most important characters in fiction cannot be so simply defined. *A's* cannot simply be the desire to divorce. *A* must have a past, an inner life, fears and desires, relationships, fantasies, preferences, tastes, habits.

Minor characters have many uses in a book besides setting the major characters in a social context. Without that social context, we may not believe. Why is this woman totally alone and totally dependent on this guy she has just met? Where are her women friends? Where's her family? If she has no friends, why not? What's wrong with her or her situation? That social context helps us understand the major characters. Why would a young girl of eleven roam the cold city streets at night – because we've given her a mother, a minor character, who is always out drinking and desperately trying to pick up a man. A character's friends can say a lot about a character, and just as much if she has no real friends at all.

Minor characters may also help to shade something in, represent alternatives the protagonist did not take, represent different choices or opinions or alternate fates. Sometimes minor characters represent other aspects of the major character, the darker or lighter side, if you will, their youth or their old age. Sometimes minor characters give local color, help to make a place real, alive, vivid. In *The Kitchen Man*, minor characters are extremely important. The protagonist, Gabriel Rose, is an aspiring playwright and a waiter in a pretentious restaurant. His friends, all fellow waiters, represent choices he does not make – Geller marries and has children; Matthew, a gay man, sleeps with his famous customers – but they also comment, freely and sarcastically, about Gabriel's choices. Besides helping to create the back-biting, late-night, gossip-fueled world of the restaurant business, one of their important functions is to help portray Gabriel as a young man who is still very dependent on other people's opinions of him. A lot of the shading in fiction depends on skillful use of minor characters. There are also the joys of the bizarre minor characters, often named as in Dickens for their grotesquerie. Sometimes the sharply drawn or amusingly caricatured minor folk are what we most fondly remember from a book. Sancho Panza. Dr. Watson. Queequeg. Merlin. Tinkerbell.

Another function of characters, whether major or minor, is to give an alternative view of each other. In *Three Women*, Suzanne, a law school professor and an appeals lawyer, sees herself as a bird of prey going after the rats of the system. Her estranged daughter Elena sees Suzanne as a fussy tight-assed woman who must micromanage everything in her life. Her best friend Marta sees her as someone who is too generous with everyone else. We begin to understand a person when we not only comprehend how that person sees herself but how others see her, both positively and negatively.

When you can't tell the minor characters apart without going back repeatedly to check their names, the story is in real trouble. In a novel, that might conceivably happen with some very minor character, although it's well to be careful in dealing with the little guys that you do inform the reader each time in some reasonably subtle way just who that character is. You can do it simply in passing, in ways such as: "Susan saw Charles coming up the steps of the porch. Loretta nodded at him and looked away. It seemed to Susan that Loretta was not pleased to see her brother coming to the house."

Sometimes, of course, you just have to bite the bullet and make a chart. In *City of Darkness, City of Light*, a novel about the French revolution, there are six viewpoint characters and a cast of thousands. The publisher asked for a Cast of Characters, a little guide, so that if you don't happen to remember as you are going along who the Bishop of Arras is, or Collot d'Herbois, the handy dandy list will remind you.

Your minor characters can be catalysts that draw out the different and sometimes conflicting emotions of your characters. Through the main character's interplay with minor characters, we get to see the protagonist in action: How does she act in relation to an authority like a boss? How does she treat a homeless guy on the street? Does she fight back when a stranger in a bar paws at her? Does she empty her bank account for a boyfriend who's been hitting her up for months? Or for a family down the street who's about to be evicted? Minor characters can serve as devices that spin your main characters into action – by making demands, by drawing them into trouble, by presenting temptations – that force your protagonist to make a revealing choice by challenging them or forcing them to react under pressure.

When you're working with your major characters before you really begin to write your story, you might want to accumulate dossiers on them. You'll want to answer many questions about these major characters, beside the obvious questions of age, sex, and physical description. You'll want to imagine them doing some characteristic action such as dancing, playing tennis; some kind of physical or mental work; you'll need to know their family and educational and class and ethnic background; and of course their name.

You might ask yourself whether they have close friends and how many? Who are their acquaintances? Their enemies? What do they seek in friends? Yes-men, siblings who mix rivalry and affection, mommas and daddies, challenges, supporters, networkers, someone who is primarily interesting because useful? What do they do when they're lonely? Turn on the TV? Call up Mom? Go down to the corner bar and have a drink? Try to pick someone up? Get stoned? Eat? Meditate? Pray? If so, to whom and for what?

What does your character do for a living and how does that person feel about working? What is their work history? What would be their fantasy job? What do they do for fun?

What happens when they are thwarted or blocked? Do they show anger? Conceal it? Swallow it? Who do they blame for their troubles? Themselves? Their mother? Blacks? Jews? The rich? Women? A hated rival? Everybody else?

Does your character identify with their mother or their father more? What kind of childhood did the character have? What do they tell themselves about their childhood (as opposed to how it was); how do they present it to others?

What is the person's relationship to objects? You might ask yourself what possessions they have and if any of their possessions mean something particular – obsessive or simply enjoyable or prideful – to them. Do they hoard? Do they have certain beloved objects we associate with them? How do they relate to technology? What kind of relationship do they have with their vehicle?

What discrepancies are interesting in the character between professed or even deeply held values and behavior? How honest is the person about those failures, to him- or herself? To others? It is in such contradictions and the way a character may handle them that we sometimes grasp their essence.

Some of these questions will be useful and some will not and so you may generate your own lists. However, I will share with you one question I find extremely useful whenever I am having difficulty entering a character. Empathy is part of the necessary equipment of any novelist who aspires to more than rewriting their own early or current history. But sometimes empathy fails. One of my own ways then is to ask of my character what is asked in the next to last position of a Tarot reading: What is most hoped for and/or most feared? Often that is a key to a character.

My last little trick for entry is to give the character some little piece of myself, some moment of my childhood or my adult life, to give it over and thus lose it. But often that little blood sacrifice works, and the character then can be entered and comes alive. Basically you enter a character wherever and whenever you can so that you can look at the world as that person sees it and sees themselves. Fiction is preeminently the art that requires both empathy and imagination. Autobiography will only carry a writer so far, maybe one good novel of youth and one of middle age, unless she or he has a truly extraordinary life or mind. Once you grant that the novelist works out of other people's lives as well as her own, you grant her a license to write about old age while in her thirties, about the loss of a child while hers are secure, or even unborn or never to be conceived, about passion out of tranquility, about ax murder and poison when she will not set a mouse trap.

Fans of a particular novel may assume the author is the protagonist. Sometimes a reader will become incensed if you explain that a particular character is not literally yourself. Sometimes such a reader will assume you are attempting to fool them; that you are a hypocrite who lacks the courage to stand up and be revealed as an ex-mental patient or a lesbian mother or whatever. The second common reaction is annoyance and disillusionment. I thought it was true and now you tell me you just made it up. We still have a Puritan mistrust of the imagination as a vehicle of truth, an unwillingness to understand that the patterns and forms of art may be true in ways that are not literal but are profound.

Successful fiction has been created out of the deeply felt stories of wolves, cats, dogs, horses, Neanderthals, intelligent arthropods, gods, beasts and robots. Sometimes the urge to fiction comes from exploring selves not lived out. I am aware of countless possibilities I did not choose, myriad alternate selves I might have become had I acted otherwise or had chance descended on me with a different leverage. The urge to fiction is, I suspect, partly the urge to explore those alternate universes of possibility. Every character I have created in every novel has some aspects of myself built in and I have lived that character while writing it. Thus even when we are writing about lives extremely different from our own, choices we will never have to make, events we will never in our own flesh experience, we can still learn a great deal about ourselves as we create and explore very different characters in fiction.

One device for giving a sense of character I have not discussed is voice. Often when I am using various viewpoints in a novel, I take care that each one has a different voice. I want it to be the case that if you pick up the novel and turn at random to a page, even if there are ten different viewpoint characters, you will instantly be able to tell from the language and the style exactly which character's mind you are in. I believe that even though I used ten viewpoints in *Gone to Soldiers*, that if you read random pages in the novel, you can tell from the voice and diction in whose viewpoint I was writing.

Often if you are using first person for a character, choices of language and style, diction and word choice are particularly important. But it is also a good idea to create this clear differentiation in third person. Take another look at the work of some of the masters of creating voice: Grace Paley, in her short stories. All Kurt Vonnegut's novels. Mark Twain's Huckleberry Finn. Barbara Kingsolver's Taylor Greer in *The Bean Trees*. But the first person voice can be especially important if you are writing a memoir.

Now if you are writing about your own life whether you give yourself a new name or write in an openly autobiographical memoir, you may think there's no problem creating characters – and certainly not in depicting yourself. Think again. Often people who are writing directly out of their own lives have more trouble trying to characterize in a sharp and memorable manner themselves or their intimates than do writers who are making up the inhabitants of Dodge City or the Orion Nebula. Whether you are writing fiction or a memoir, the means of characterization available to you are the same. Much of what I have written about characterization in fiction applies to writing personal narrative just as strongly. Once again, deep characterization methods include the uses of a character's fears, anxiety, desires, passions, attachments to things and to people, friendships and antipathies, real beliefs. It's a problem when someone writing about themselves fails to imagine themselves as a character; that kind of writing makes the assumption that character development is not important, that the reader knows all about them, because of course, the writer does.

As we have mentioned, it is a problem when you are writing about your life if you do not understand the other characters you are presenting to us and their motives for acting as they did, but it is not insurmountable. Mary Gordon's memoir about her father, *The Shadow Man*, is a piece of detective work, an account of trying to understand who he was. She attempted to discover his family background, the forces that distorted him, his real life. It is the quest to understand her father that is the moving force of her story.

You must characterize yourself without appearing to set yourself up as a martyr or a saint. You have to make yourself real as a character, which may require backing off a bit and trying to see yourself clearly. Readers often bristle when writers present themselves as victims. Having been deeply hurt, offended, wrongfully treated, as we all have been at times, it's difficult to avoid conveying self-pity. It's harder still to be even-handed, to see different sides of an event or relationship. Sometimes a person had no hand whatsoever in their misfortune. So how are they to write about it? There are probably as many answers as there are writers who take the time to solve the problem, but there are some techniques worth mentioning. One is humor.

Sometimes we can catch readers off-guard if we can make them laugh at situations that, treated in a more straightforward way, might seem self-serving or self-pitying. In one of our classes a woman presented a piece that, in the hands of a less skilled writer, might have sounded like your typical my-husband-left-me-for-a-younger-woman story. Except that she compared her husband's new wife to a white lab rat and kept the metaphor alive (including references to her spare, vegetarian diet; her quick, nervous movements) until the class was in stitches.

Writers who take on the Holocaust have every reason to portray themselves as victims, yet in the hands of a brilliant memoirist like Primo Levi, a story may be as much about the complex social hierarchy of all the prisoners around him, and thus become even deeper in its implications. It is difficult to remember that in any horrible situation, there are other things going on at the same time as the horror. People like and dislike each other; power struggles develop; petty resentments do not disappear. Writing about these other aspects will not dissipate the horror but might make it all the more real. *The Diary of Anne Frank* is especially moving because each member of the two families hiding is not a helpless lamb, but a person with sometimes quite selfish human needs.

The oldest chestnut of the creative writing class is *show, don't tell*. Make a scene in which an action unfolds, rather than simply report it. In attempting to avoid writing as a victim, making the decision to allow a situation to unfold in a scene permits your readers to participate in the situation and make up their own minds about its implications. Stating, "My father was an irresponsible drunk" might be less effective than writing a scene in which a father comes home singing on Christmas eve with an armful of pies and then, drunk as a lord, falls down the stairs, crushing the special dessert. It's well to remember that as a child we may have been miserable, but we didn't always think of ourselves as victims while the situation was unfolding. We were sometimes focused on those pies. Sometimes there were other people being treated the same way, bothers, sisters, and we were thinking of them. Or strategizing about how to save ourselves. But we may not have been thinking then what we now know as adults: that Dad was a beast.

In Frank McCourt's *Angela's Ashes*, it was a given to the children that their father was a drunk. They didn't necessarily think of dad as evil, but as dad; that's how he was. They thought about food and play and mom and the neighbors and how to grab a banana from the corner store. One of the reasons *Angela's Ashes* kept so many people riveted, instead of throwing the book aside in despair, was the author's ability to keep the reader with him. He used humor. He used language. He certainly created a memorable voice. He created vivid scenes that allowed the reader to become involved in the action, to live and breathe the world of Limerick, to go back in time, where a less skilled writer might have simply poured on the despair. Little Frank was not a victim. He was a kid whose father was a drunk and whose early life was one of intense desire: for food, for warmth, for peace between his parents.

Again, beware of self-hatred as well as self-aggrandizement. If you come off in your reminiscences of childhood as self-satisfied, boring and predictable, we will not want to read about you. Further, if all the other characters only exist to admire or abuse you, we will speedily lose interest in them. They must have a life of their own. In some of the most successful memoirs, other characters are extremely important and vividly drawn. Lillian Hellman built *Pentimento* around other characters, with each section of the book named for one of them.

In many ways it does not matter whether you are writing a novel or short story or memoir: the devices of characterization are pretty much the same. The characters must be vivid and differentiated whether they are invented or your own Aunt Sharon and Uncle Jack. In one case, you must turn your imagination loose; in the other, you must mine memory for the richest scraps of observation and recollection, ways of speaking, ways of being in the room and in the world. When you're writing a memoir, you might want to accumulate a simpler dossier on each of your major characters than you need in fiction, a dossier that consists of everything you can remember about the person, and what other family members and friends may remember, if you ask.

Although we'll address the implications of writing about families and relatives in another chapter, it is quite true that in some cases, especially if information on them is not available to you, you may have to re-imagine them (attempting to be true to your recollections as well as your knowledge of their motivations, desires, etc.) before they become successful characters. Since you don't know all about them (remembering them, for example, from the vantage point of childhood), you'll have to re-invent them at different stages in their lives. You'll have to ask some of the same questions about your great grandfather when he was twenty, that you'd ask about any character.

There are in any life a great many minor characters, major of course in their own lives, but minor in the one you are writing about. Sometimes it is necessary to meld some of these people together into one person, for the sake of simplicity and to avoid introducing too many characters and confusing the reader. You could make your two best friends in college into one confidant. I remember reading a memoir about a stroke survivor in which she explained she had turned several of the friends who had helped her while she was recovering into one person, for convenience in telling her story.

One very important way of characterizing your people is by the language a character speaks, the way they use words, their use of jargon or inflated or rough language, what they say and do not say. Often you remember someone as much by the way they spoke as by any other salient point about them. If you can give that flavor to their speech, you are on the way toward creating a person that the reader will believe in.

In writing about ourselves, there is something that we shouldn't forget. It is not uncommon that someone will be a very lively talker, full of anecdotes and lively language and comparisons that startle you or make you smile. But sometimes when that very person sits down to write about their life, instead of writing with flavor and energy, they write in a flat boring manner. They leave out all the juicy details and the local color and give us a sort of abstract summing up that has no life to it. It's not clear why this happens. It may be that a certain inner censor comes into play, which says to the writer, "Oh, you can't include that!" Or, "Get on with the story. That detail isn't important. Who are you to take up so many pages, anyhow?" Or perhaps the situation is so very real to the writer that she feels her reader will somehow automatically see what she sees, hear what she hears, because of course, it's all there so vividly in her mind. Maybe it's pure embarrassment. "My God! I can't really tell people what the other waiters and I used to call the customers who stiffed us for a tip." Whatever the reason, the writing lacks all flavor and originality. It sounds like the kind of writing you find in the manual for your VCR. Remember, the language you write most definitely characterizes you for the reader.

Creating Characters: the Dossier

We fill out this questionnaire with every major character we create. We suggest you key it on to your computer or make photocopies for later use. Answering these questions in full (and adding any that are helpful to you or more specific to your project) leads to the creation of a rich and useful record of physical, emotional and historical information; information that the reader may never see but that will send your imagination digging into surprisingly fertile new places. For minor characters, you might want to answer only some of these questions. For people in your memoirs, people you assume you know well, you'll be impressed how creative speculation can make a familiar person come to life on the page.

- Name:

- What do they most like to be called:

- Do they have a name that they most resent being called? Who has called them by this name:

- Age:

- Physical appearance:

- Way of dressing:

- How does your character feel about his or her face and body?

- When your character thinks about his or her body or face, what are they most vain about?

- What would they most like to change about their physical appearance?

- Voice and/or accent:

- Kind of laugh?

- Do they sing? With others? Alone? In the shower? What do they sing?

- Where were they born? What city?

- Where do they live now? Why? Do they like it?

- What events going on in the world when they were little were adults most likely to talk about when they sat having coffee?

- Where and how educated?

- Are they proud or ashamed of their education? Have they ever lied about it?

- Occupation?

- Is that what the person expected to be doing at this point in his or her life? Did they expect to be better off or worse?

- Is that what their parents expected of them?

- What did their parents urge them/influence them to do?

- At what age did the person first work? What was the job?

- What was the best and worst job the person ever held? Why?

- What would be their fantasy job?

- What kind of vehicle if any does the person drive?

- Where do they live? How do they feel about where they live?

- Married? Living with someone? Who?
  Children? Living with them or not?

- Were their parents happy together when they were born? Later?

- When they were growing up, did their parents argue? About what?

- Siblings?

- Current relationship with parents and/or siblings?

- Other important relatives (aunts, uncles, cousins, grandparents)?

- Which of these relatives were the most important for good or ill?

- Which relative did the child hear that he or she looked like, and how did they feel about that comparison?

- First experience of death in or out of the family?

- Something happened to your character when they were young, perhaps in grade school that they are embarrassed about to this day. What occurred?

- Who is your character's best friend, if they have one?

- If they were to confide in someone, who would it be? A friend? Bartender? Family member? Religious leader? Doctor? Therapist? Stranger?

- If you surprised your character in the street, where might they be going that they would least want you to know about?

- What does he or she do when angry?

- What does he or she do when depressed?

- What is your character's most closely guarded secret?

- If your character could undo one thing they have done in their life, what would that be?

- If they could have any wish, what would they get?

- What do they do for fun or amusement or to unwind?

- Favorite food or type of meal?

- Set your character in motion across a room and describe how he or she moves.

- What is the most physical thing that they do regularly (work out; walk; dance; clean the house; have sex; play touch football)?

- Do they have any pets? Did they as a child?

- If they had the power to hurt anyone without punishment, whom would they hurt?

- What is their biggest fear? Their most irrational fear?

- What do they resent most that another person did to them or caused to happen to them?

- What is their religious affiliation, if any?

- What do they really believe in?

- Have they ever had a nickname? As a child? As an adult? How did they feel about that nickname, and how did they acquire it?

- How often do they fall in love and what happens?

- Do they have a physical or character type they repeatedly engage?

- Fantasy life? Content and frequency of daydreaming?

The Image Game

I play a game with workshop classes often, particularly in poetry or fiction workshops, but sometimes also in personal narrative. It is a game about imagery, obviously applicable to poetry, but it relates well to prose as a tool in the development of character. Usually I have people divide into groups unless the class is quite small. First I have them play the game on paper. I ask them to think of someone they know or even a fictional person, and to answer as many of the following questions as they can. For instance, they are not to answer the "vehicle" question with the car the person actually drives, but rather with what kind of car that person *is*. This is a variation on an old parlor game called Botticelli, but I introduce it for a reason. After they have finished, I have each member of the class read their results to each other.

I want the feedback from the other people in the group to run along the lines of, is this person being described male or female, old or young, and what is the attitude being conveyed by the imagery: someone the writer admires, likes or loves, dislikes, disapproves of or has an ambivalent attitude toward? What are the characteristics conveyed (dynamic, passive, vibrant, reclusive, angry, calm)? I ask the writer to consider whether they have put across what they wanted to by their choice of imagery.
The image game:

If this person were an animal, what kind of animal would he or she be?

What kind of bird?

What kind of fish?

What kind of musical instrument?

What color?

What holiday?

What room?

What building or type of building?

What kind of noise?

What article of clothing?

What era in history?

What piece of furniture?

What tool?

What TV program?

What kind of meal?

What kind of game?

What dance?

What book or kind of book?

What smell?

What country (or what kind of landscape) would he or she be?

What kind or make of car?

Which flower?

Which fruit?

Which vegetable?

Which tree?

What kind of weather?

What season?

I ask the workshop to keep in mind that while this is not a predominant way of creating a character, using certain imagery can subtly influence our reaction to that character and make it far more vivid, real and convincing to us. Sometimes simply associating a particular color or animal imagery with a character gives us clues to him or her and creates expectations the reader will experience without pinning down what is causing the reaction. It's just a little exercise in a different way of thinking about character that I often do at the beginning of a unit or lecture on characterization. Besides, most people find it fun to do. There's no down side to that.

4

The Uses of Dialogue

ONE OF THE MOST FOOLISH mistakes a prose writer can make is to overlook the uses of dialogue. To ignore what dialogue can do for you is analogous to using a computer with a 20 gigabyte hard drive as nothing more than a typewriter; why only write letters with a tool that can run your entire house? Because a play or a movie script looks like it's entirely made of dialogue, it's easy to assume that dialogue is more important for the playwright or screenwriter than the writer of prose. It's also easy to think that dialogue is simple, just a couple of people talking.

To the extent that there are rules of dialogue in writing fiction or the personal narrative, they are a loose set. In the same way that writers of stream-of-consciousness do away with conventional sentence structure, some writers disregard conventional methods of punctuation. They don't use quotation marks; they may not use a new paragraph for each speaker; they use colons or em-dashes to introduce a speech. Although this is not wise, it is not illegal. It's a writer's style, a personal issue. There is no Great White English Teacher in the sky, with a bolt of lightning in one hand and a red pencil in the other. The only really important rule is this: The dialogue has to work in context – meaning, on the most basic level, that the reader always has to know who is speaking and what they are saying. (This is not as obvious as it sounds.) On a more advanced level, it means that once you understand what dialogue can do, it will become a vehicle you can employ to carry some of the load of your story telling.

Many writers of non-fiction, of memoirs and autobiographical novels, write long passages of absolutely boring and sometimes incoherent dialogue. Then they justify the mess by saying, "But this is exactly what people sound like." Or worse, "I taped it."

Having a good ear means writing dialogue that *sounds* idiomatic. Just because you are writing about things that happened, does not mean you want to transcribe the way people actually speak. If you have ever listened to a tape of a normal conversation, you will hear a great many repetitions, interruptions, non-sequiturs and unfinished sentences. Conversation typically meanders, repeats, meanders some more.

People spend an enormous amount of time talking about the weather, about how-are-you, about television and what they had for lunch and nothing at all. There is a time for banal conversation, mostly when you want to reassure someone that you are sympathetic, that you mean that person no harm. But your book is rarely the place for an exact transcription of human speech. You're a writer, not a courtroom stenographer. There are very skillful writers who describe people's dreary lives in what would appear to be the most commonplace exchanges, but Ann Beatty and Harold Pinter have labored long and hard to construct dialogue that sounds as if it was lifted from an elevator and, in point of fact, is highly compressed and worked over. Lillian Ross, the legendary New Yorker magazine interviewer, regularly made her subjects sound like egomaniacal boors by seemingly transcribing what they said. In fact, as the novelist Irving Wallace observed about her book on Hemingway, Ross was "selectively listening and viewing, capturing the one moment that entirely illumines the scene, fastening on the one quote that tells all."

What you are doing with so-called realistic dialogue is creating the illusion of idiomatic speech. What you are really doing is creating highly edited, highly selective representations of human speech.

In the novel *Storm Tide*, the main character, David Green, meets Stumpy Squeer, somewhat retarded but the kind of fellow that can live comfortably in the small town where he grew up because people watch after him. Rather than introduce Stumpy as an inarticulate mumbler, which might have been closer to a real life portrait, we decided to choose dialogue that infused him with some pride and purpose:

Stumpy was short and thick, fifty more or less, with barrel-like haunches that made him seem to roll forward as he walked.

Judith stood on the steps, "Let's go, you guys! Gordon. David. Lunch!"

"Will you join us, Stumpy?" Gordon's voice was deep and courtly.

Stumpy shook his head no.

"Going to get back to your book?" Gordon asked him. "Stumpy's been working on one for three years now."

"Four," Stumpy said.

"Really?" I loved the idea. Stumpy Squeer, hermit savant. "What are you writing about?"

"Not writin'. Been readin' it," he said. "Almost finished, too."

In good writing, fiction or non-fiction, dialogue always exists to make a point, preferably many points at once. Most importantly, dialogue characterizes the speaker. Because the reader takes note of everything a character says, the reader will develop attitudes about that character. Dialogue also gives the reader the illusion of discovery. Remember that old chestnut of Creative Writing 101? Show, don't tell? Dialogue is the perfect vehicle for showing action unfolding or a character's attitude changing in a scene. Moreover, the information learned through a conversation might register more deeply than the information the author narrates, because the reader feels she has overheard the characters say it and thus discovered it by herself. If I recounted a conversation in which a Hollywood producer, ten minutes into our first telephone call, guaranteed me an executive producer's credit for a film on a book he had not yet read and offered to buy me a hundred shares of a hot stock to boot, you wouldn't trust him any more than I did. Yet all you knew about him was what came out of his mouth, his dialogue.

In English due to the French overlay on the Anglo-Saxon, and the Latinate and Greek derived words over those layers, we have levels of formality. So, in order to describe what you do for a living, you can either say:

"I sequence the genetic blue print of the Drosophila melanogaster."

Or,

"I map fruit fly genes."

The use of formality versus informality in speech, the use of colorful idioms, the use of slang and obscenities, the misuse of words, all tell you something about the character who is speaking. Obviously, the choice of formal speech versus slang may tip off the reader to that character's level of education, even his pretensions. Further, when that character chooses to use formal speech, or with whom they use it, may provide insight into him or her.

I knew a man who was college educated, well read and articulate. He worked in a white-collar profession. But when he spoke with blue-collar or service-trades people in a pizza joint, at an auto repair shop, his language reverted to a tough guy movie parody. It might be that the man was insecure, so that his personality mirrored those to whom he spoke; or perhaps his background was somewhat less middle class than he liked to let on. Without telling your readers what to think, they are developing theories of their own. In *Storm Tide*, the character Crystal tells different stories of her past to different people. Characters in books, exactly like people we know in life, are not one-dimensional but complex and sometimes contradictory in their actions and intentions. We can convey that in our dialogue.

Mastering the jargon of particular professions is always important to a writer. Too much jargon can be unintelligible, but English contains many sub-languages, and mastering them can make your piece seem more real. Not that you will ever really have to write exactly as a lawyer or a geneticist or an arson detective would speak, but you should master enough of their idiom to create the impression of such a person.

Many of the submissions we get at the press sound artificial. People think, because they've seen TV shows about every conceivable kind of character, that they can write those characters. But without the writer taking the time to learn about them, they are seldom rendered as more than caricatures and types. We have read manuscripts in which trials were unconvincing because the writer never bothered to witness one, except in TV dramas; novels in which the police behaved in ways any simple review of procedures with a knowledgeable officer would have fixed.

When writing about the conversation between you and another person, one that actually happened, you'd have to have an eidetic memory or a tape recorder to get that conversation exactly. Happily, that's the last thing you want to do, even in a memoir. You want to imply what a person conveyed and how they said it; shorten the conversation and get to the point. In the memoir *Rookie Cop*, the writer, a police spy, actually wore a body wire, saved the transcriptions of his tapes, and was in the rare position of being able to provide a word-for-word account of his attempt to draw information out of a suspect. One conversation meandered for thirteen pages in first draft and was so full of meaningless exchanges and in-jokes as to render it unintelligible, however accurate. We had to cut it down to a half-page in which the flavor of the cat and mouse exchange was preserved and the important information was efficiently delivered.

Writers who equate reality with transcriptions of speech have similar problems with dialect: Black English, for example, and the various forms of rural English, English that has a Yiddish or a Spanish flavor. How realistically should you portray the dialect you are working with? You want people to read and understand what you have written. You do not want to erect an impenetrable wall of dialect between the reader and your work. I must have seen the classic reggae outlaw movie *The Harder They Come* about ten times, and if I did not catch every word of the Kingston, Jamaica patois, I was carried along with the action, the setting, the music. When I picked up a novel written (by an American) in the same dead-accurate patois, I could not penetrate it and simply gave up trying. No one can give you a formula for dealing with this problem; it's a question of style and may vary from work to work. Flavor is what you are after, not the exact pronunciation of a dialect so thick no reader will be able to understand it. Many good African-American writers demonstrate mastery of the levels of idiom and dialect from street jive to commencement address formal, as the demands of the piece and the situation warrant.

In the novel, *Woman on the Edge of Time*, Connie Ramos, a Chicana woman, is drawn to the door of her New York apartment:

"It's me, Dolly!" Her niece was screaming in the hall. "Let me in! Hurry!"

"Momento." Connie fumbled with the bolt, the police lock, finally swinging the door wide. Dolly fell in past her, her face bloody. Connie clutched at Dolly, trying to see how badly she was hurt. "Que pasa? Who did this?"

The author is using only a few Spanish words to give us the flavor of the speaker. Another way to use foreign phrases is to quickly and unobtrusively translate them:

> The waiter bowed. "Encore du café, Monsieur?"
> I nodded and he filled my cup with thick black coffee.

It is obvious that if you are writing historical fiction, you want to avoid anachronisms. Remember, the farther back you go, the less accurate will be your rendition of the language and the more you will be simply creating an illusion of eighteenth-century language for example. If you get too sucked in to writing the language of the period, you will produce something quaint and curious and mostly devoid of interest to modern readers. That verisimilitude is the reason few readers we know actually made their way through *Mason-Dixon*, Thomas Pynchon's recent novel, even when they had devoured his previous superlative work.

I had this problem recently in my novel *City of Darkness, City of Light* about the French Revolution. I had to figure out how to convey the highly idiomatic, somewhat secretive, often obscene and usually colorful language of the *sans culottes*, the Parisian working class of the revolution. I realized that the nearest equivalent in modern language would be Black ghetto speech. But I also realized after I had played with this, that it would simply render my attempt to give verisimilitude to eighteenth-century life, ideas, manners, the absolute quietus. Nobody would believe these were people talking in 1792. So I gave up that idea and produced dialogue not nearly as slangy as the actual language and not nearly as obscene or colorful.

Realistic dialogue, no matter how accurate, is not always what you are aiming for. If you are writing science fiction, your characters should not sound like your neighbors. You would want to give an alien flavor to their speech. Flavor is the key word. It has to be intelligible. All aliens speak English or you have no story, unless your story is about the difficulty or inability to communicate from one culture to another. Similarly, if you are writing about your aged grandfather from the old country, he should not use current slang or up-to-date idioms. But neither should he, if he arrived on a passenger ship from Italy, speak exactly as he did when he got off the ship. His speech has to be understandable.

Dialogue also reveals character in what someone is trying to do with what they choose to say. Is your character using words to flatter? To lie? To provoke guilt? The words that you put in a character's mouth inform our opinion about that character. Those words tell us how a character acts, the way their mind works, what they want without the author telling us.

We were having an idle conversation about our car breaking down some years ago when an assistant of ours said, "My girlfriend and I think you should get a BMW." A helpful enough comment at face value. But what did her dialogue reveal? That outside of work, she and her partner bothered to think about us (we didn't do much thinking about them); but more importantly to us, that they viewed us as having a hell of a lot more money than we had.

Although dialogue can reveal deep character, silence can be equally revealing.

"You were not with her?"

He sighed. "So I'm a couple of hours late. What do you want, proof?"

"Because if I ever found out."

"I would never lie to you. Period."

"She's my best friend, Bob. The only friend I've made in this town."

"I was hunting with Reggie. We got a late start back and spent the night in a motel. I can show you the receipt, for Christ sake." He dug into his wallet. "Do you want to see it?"

"Reggie is in Milwaukee. He called looking for you an hour ago. His plane was delayed."

He rubbed his hand across his forehead, staring into his drink.

"Bob? Did you hear me? I said Reggie called."

He remained in his chair, staring down.

It is not necessary to have pages and pages of dialogue, and in fact it is in general not a great idea to do so. You can give the meat of a scene in a few exchanges. In fact, you pass hours, days, years, of time. Here, the passages of time are italicized.

I called my agent *just after mailing off the manuscript*: "I think it's the best thing I've ever written."

"I look forward to reading it *this weekend*," he said.

Exactly *three weeks later*, I gave him a call. "What do you think?"

He brushed me off. "I need some more time with it."

I called again *in a month*, this time after a stiff drink. "He's in a meeting," his secretary said. "He'll call you back."

He never did. *Two weeks later*, I strode into his office. I was not new to this game. The longer they took with their response, the worse they thought of the book. It was back to teaching, if I could get a job after all this time. Just keep your dignity, I told myself, grasping the side of his desk to keep my hands from shaking. "Tell it to me straight," I said.

"I have to be honest with you." My agent could not meet my eyes. "We've looked everyplace. I think we've lost the damn thing."

You notice that each line of dialogue has a tag. Tags are vital. Now the most common tags, *he said, she said*, are dull but also transparent. That is, the reader tends to ignore them, to use them simply as markers. Sometimes each speaker is distinct enough. Identified either through their speech patterns or the content of their arguments, the reader always knows who is speaking, even in a long exchange. It is important always to check your dialogue and make sure the reader never has to go back and count lines to figure out who is saying what. That breaks the flow; takes the reader out of the story. A participant in one of our writing classes told us that in her daughter's school there was a chart listing all the verbs you should substitute for *said*. Remember they also told us that sitting under our desks with our heads between our knees would protect us from the atom bomb. Likely, they wanted to inject a little action into the children's writing. Don't get too fancy, as in:

"Hello, little girl," expostulated the wolf. "Where are you going?" he interrogated her.

Action or description tags (in italics below) are great, because they set the words into the scene. They attach the words to bodies, moving or still, and allow us to see as well as hear the characters.

From *Three Women*:

She wakened curled in the backseat to find that Chad was checking them into a motel. They all fell into the bed and more or less slept until it got noisy in the morning. Then they all took turns in the shower and Chad shaved.

"How come you aren't shaving?" she asked Evan.

"I'm going to grow a beard. Great disguise. I look older with five o'clock shadow."

She made a disgusted grimace. "Just don't expect me to kiss you!"

He grabbed her and rubbed his cheek against hers. "Kiss, kiss, kiss."

They were both giggling as they fell on the bed. *Chad came in whistling.* "Leave you guys alone for five minutes and you're at it. In permanent heat, that's what you are."

Elena said, "I think we should all do something to change our appearance."

Chad shrugged. "Who's looking for three kids. Runaways are a dime a dozen."

"Your father's going to want his car back."

Chad waved that away with an airy gesture. "We'll have to ditch it at some point and get another."

"Oh, sure. We can trade," Evan said. "Hi, want to trade your old Ford Escort for a nice BMW, no questions asked?"

"For the time being, let's get as far as we can in it."

"I've never been to California," *Elena said, curled up again in the backseat with a bag of potato chips that would do for breakfast.*

They walked around the mall until the traffic thinned out. Finally, Chad saw what he was waiting for. A guy pulled up in a dark blue Ford Taurus. His girlfriend was waiting in the passenger's seat while he ran into the liquor store. He left the engine running.

Chad yanked open the door on the passenger's side. "Out." *He shoved the gun into her neck.*

"Don't hurt me!'

"Don't scream, or I'll shoot. I don't want you, just the car." *He pulled her out.* "Evan, drive." Evan flung the backpack behind him and fumbled for the parking brake.

Chad motioned Elena into the backseat, and they lurched off. "Okay, Elena. Where do we go?"

"Turn right at the light." *She turned on the overhead and looked at the map Evan had bought.* "Okay, just keep going. We're heading for the interstate."

61

You should also be aware of the uses of Direct versus Indirect Dialogue. Direct dialogue shows us your characters speaking. Indirect dialogue (in italics below) sums up what they said.

> When I last saw Rebecca again, it was in the elevator of a New York hotel. *Attempting to hide, I mumbled hello.* "This is the most amazing coincidence," she said. "How long has it been? We must have dinner. Come up to my room for a drink. I'll call Mom," she added, as if, five years after our divorce I still referred to her mother that way. *I said that I was only here for a sales conference and would be leaving that evening.* "Oh come now. You can't stay a few hours more?"
>
> *I shook my head, Sorry,* and Rebecca fixed me that disbelieving stare. "Oh, yes. I imagine. . . Doreen is it?. . . would be absolutely incapable of spending another evening without you." *When I said I had to get back because someone was house sitting the cats,* Rebecca glowed with sudden victory. "You're no longer married, are you?"

Indirect dialogue has a flattening effect that can be used for irony, humor, distancing, or to diminish the importance of one speaker in order to emphasize the other. It can also be used to summarize action or information the reader already knows and that you don't want to slow down the action by repeating.

> "Good morning, Mr. Chalmers," said the principal of my fourth school in as many years. *I began my story, but he simply glanced at the fat file folder on his desk and told me not to bother.*

In the next example, an unimportant character is created by indirect dialogue. What matters here is the type of case economic pressure is forcing Suzanne to take on, rather than the particulars of this client.

From *Three Women*:

> It was not a case she wanted. She contained herself, listening, questioning him, taking careful notes with Jaime backing her up. Bud Hiller had inquired coldly who Jaime was upon entering her office, but now it was as if Jaime were a cat on a chair. . . .
>
> *Hiller orated on, his injuries, the stinginess of his dead father, the*

perfidy of his siblings and their spouses, how his previous lawyers had failed him and his just cause. She listened, she took notes, and she thought how she would love to show him the door, but this case leaked money through all its flimsy seams. She had come to a financial cross-roads where she must take cases that would pay her bills instead of cases that excited her legally or ethically. She was still the litigator she had always been. She could find a new angle to use. She began to plot her strategy in getting Bud his money and doing his siblings out of theirs.

Unless someone is telling a story, a very involving story, watch out for long speeches. Even if someone is giving a speech in a story, you can give the flavor of the speech in a paragraph or give us some important highlights, interspersed with reaction. Dull dialogue is a much commoner problem than too much repartee, but that also can carry a book astray if it gets out of hand.

In novels and memoirs and stories writers might choose to use no direct dialogue at all, while others rely heavily on dialogue. Again, there are no hard and fast rules. Dialogue can hasten the unfolding of your story by revealing elements of the plot that the reader and/or the other characters do not know. It allows the reader to believe she is making up her own mind about a character, because she is judging the character in action, on the character's own merits, rather than being told by the author what to think. The use of dialogue makes it easy to create dramatic scenes that alternate with straight narration, and thereby show the action of a story enfolding.

The Exercise

In no more than one page, create an interaction between two characters, written entirely in dialogue, attempting to use all three of the techniques illustrated previously:

1. Using dialogue to pass time.

2. Using action or descriptive tags

3. Using indirect dialogue.

You can create a situation of your own choosing, or use one the following situations. (Remember that when one speaker wants something the other does not, there may be an interesting element of dramatic tension in the dialogue.)

A worried parent tries to convince their child that her (or his) boyfriend (or girlfriend) is a bad choice.

A person who can no longer stand living with his/her roommate is trying to suggest that the roommate move out of the apartment they share.

A diner in a high-priced restaurant finds a worm in his salad and wants his dinner free; the management finds his request excessive.

Two people who dated twenty years ago meet by chance at a conference. One would like the relationship to resume. The other is not convinced.

A taxicab pulls over for a fare at rush hour. Two New Yorkers reach it at the same moment, each attempting to convince the other they need it more.

A very persistent guy at a bar sits next to you and suggests you get to know each other. That's the last thing on your mind.

You're home for Christmas. You really want to please your mom, whom you haven't seen in a long time. She is anxious for you to meet, and like, her new boyfriend, who not only has politics opposite yours but talks about them aggressively.

The guy in the upstairs apartment has come home from work at 2 A.M. again and pumps his stereo up full blast. This has got to stop and you go upstairs to tell him so.

5

Plot in the Novel

TRUE STORY: I know a writer who told me he needed a motel room to start his novel. What he would do was push all the furniture to the middle of the room, then cover all four walls floor to ceiling with blank paper. He would then proceed to outline his book chapter by chapter to the end, listing every incident in a flow chart. He thought visually, he told me. He needed to see it all written out on paper. Ideally, he would sequester himself in the room with pots of coffee and finger food for however long it took. When finished, he would have the book entirely worked out. All he would then have to do was transcribe the incidents to his laptop; fill in description and dialogue. I was skeptical but kept my mouth shut. Every writer I know has a different way of going about it. A friend who writes novels as well as for Hollywood, writes at night, sometimes all night, beginning after dinner and typing until dawn with the TV blasting for company. A Pulitzer Prize winner we know wrote his first three novels on the Long Island Railroad, commuting to his job in New York City. He liked to roughly sketch every scene on a different index card and then fully compose it on a legal pad. Now he's the chairman of a writing department and has an oak-paneled office overlooking a lake. Still starts with the index cards.

It wasn't the motel room that worried me about the outline man; or the days of powdered doughnuts and coffee. It was the idea that he could completely control the story without involving himself in the inner lives of his characters. He wanted to control every speech, all the action and reaction like a puppeteer, ignoring the process of entering his characters' states of consciousness and experiencing the world through them. He wanted to by-pass the mystery of the writing process, the frightening walk down unknown roads.

The danger of over-plotting, of imagining that you can entirely avoid the unknown and list the elements of a novel like the ingredients of a recipe is perhaps as dangerous as jumping into a project without a clue. Of course there are writers who do just that. Some fine writers start with a piece of blank paper and nothing more.

A large number of the submissions that we receive at the press every year are by young men who believe their adolescent experiences are the stuff of great fiction. There are a lot of scenes in bars; a lot in bedrooms – not sex scenes, but in bed, trying to decide why they should stub out their cigarettes and get up. The problem is, that besides bitching about their jobs, school, women, their parents, they have very little to say; nothing happens. After ten pages maybe a friend will come over, and start bitching about jobs, school, women, their parents. Thinking about plot beforehand can help a writer avoid the problem of starting with only a vague idea, of nothing happening, of getting to page fifty and feeling "written out" without a thing left to say.

All writers face the problem of how to shape their ideas and experiences into a form that maximizes meaning and dramatic tension, that seduces a reader into wanting to turn the page. This is obvious for writers of fiction. However, people who have their own stories to tell, of a life full of incident, sometimes imagine that all they have to do is remember their stories and type them up. Then they wonder where they've gone wrong; why editors reject their work and their very exciting lives, why even friends find reading their output makes for tough going. Because the issues of developing a narrative strategy are somewhat different for writers of memoir and autobiography, we've devoted another chapter to personal narrative. But for those who choose to fictionalize their life's adventures, however close to the truth, they too need a plot.

To make a very simplistic analogy, just because you have a car it doesn't mean you can start it up and get where you're going. Some people have a great sense of direction; most people need a map. The plot is your map. Some writers plot out the book from start to finish and know their ending before they begin. Some writers have only a vague idea of the ending, plot a few chapters ahead of themselves, take stock of where they are, how their characters will react to the situations they find themselves in, and plot out a few more until they find the ending. There is no right or wrong way to go about it. But both of us need to have some idea where we're going when we start out, so we don't waste months of our time and reams of paper.

Plot is the element of fiction most often in disrepute. It is considered by certain critics that truly serious fiction should somehow be free of this basic element of every story. But you dispense with it at your own risk. It is so basic to the narrative impulse that even a simple tale that has no characterization beyond labeling (the prince, the princess, the wicked witch) is nonetheless identifiable as fiction because it tells a story.

One basic plot is The Quest. Simply put, the main character wants something and sets out to get it. They can lose some thing and need to get it back. They can feel they are lacking something and set out to achieve it. They can be hired to take it away from somebody else. They can be commissioned to discover it. This concept – the protagonist wants something and sets out to get it – seems almost too basic to include in an essay for people who are educated enough to have undertaken serious fiction writing, but we are continually amazed, as we plow through stacks of submissions, how many writers fail to begin by asking the most basic question: What does your main character yearn for? What do they want? What sets them in motion?

Take Little Red Riding Hood. (Fairy tales and myths are often as sophisticated structurally as they are symbolically and deserve serious study.) She's given a mission: Take this basket to grandma. Think about it. Would there be a story at all if she never left the house? What if she set out to go to grandma's and made it there without incident? No trickery, no wolf, no story.

Now you could of course write the story of a little girl who never leaves the kitchen. You could write the story of a little girl getting to grandma's and having lunch. Who's going to stop you? Such a story would not rely on plot; you'd have to employ other elements to keep the reader turning pages. Description: the careful poetic description of the rare forest flora. Character insight: Riding Hood hates her mother and longs to be reunited with her absent father and grandma is her only confidante. Lively dialogue: "Grandma," Riding Hood takes the old woman's hand, "you're so frail. The doctor says you may not make it through the night. Tell me, Grandma. How can we best honor you, with burial or cremation? What is your wish?" Grandma musters the last of her strength and shrugs. "Surprise me."

You will want to employ *all* these elements in your writing: description, character insight, dialogue. But you do not want to ignore the element of plot.

Think about *The Odyssey*. In its most basic form: Ulysses wants to get home. Obstacles get in his way: Some really bad weather; Polyphemus, the Cyclops; Calypso, who saves and seduces him; Circe, the enchantress who turns Odysseus' men into swine; the Sirens, those sea nymphs who sing Odysseus' men into a trance; the lotus eaters. This is a plot as good today as it was 2800 years ago. In his novel *The Wanderers*, Sol Yurick transformed returning soldiers in a modern version of *The Anabasis* (a Greek classic about the retreat of an army in hostile territory) into an urban street gang encountering cops and rival gangs as they cross New York neighborhoods on their way back to their home turf in Brooklyn. The reason for obstacles, of course, is to enable your readers to see your characters in action, under stress, making choices either right or wrong, that will determine the outcome of the story and their lives.

The very simplest way to begin thinking about the plot is this: First, figure out who your main character, or protagonist, is. Develop her dramatic need. Then, figure out obstacles to get in her way. This yearning need not be obvious to the reader, or even to the protagonist herself, but you've got to know what it is. Nor is a character in a novel so simple as to want only one thing. But there is often one desire, however difficult it may be to pin down, that is more central than all the rest. In Dorothy Allison's novel, *Bastard Out of Carolina*, the main desire of the protagonist, a teenager named Bone, is to be loved by her mother. She isn't aware enough of herself to articulate this. She's a richly drawn character, a complex young woman. The obstacle to that love is the abusive man that her mother is sexually obsessed with as well as the grinding poverty in which the family lives (and of course because of that poverty, the lack of choices the family has).

In a detective story, the dramatic need may be to find the murderer or the evidence; the witness or even something meaningless. The Maltese

Falcon is the object of every character's desire in Dashiell Hammet's famous noir mystery novel of the same name. But what is it exactly? Why is it so desirable? The author tells us that it is a fabulously valuable gold statuette of a falcon, created as tribute for the Holy Roman Emperor Charles IV, but not many readers really give a damn. It's the action that rivets their attention, not the statue. If you say the Maltese Falcon is hot stuff, then the reader believes it's hot stuff. The movie director Alfred Hitchcock called such objects "the macguffin," a made up name for a made up thing, the sole object of which is to create a yearning that will propel characters into motion, make them want to overcome all obstacles to get it. In fantasy or science fiction, you are free to invent anything you can render believable; nonsensical elements in plot work just fine. You want space travel? Invent the warp engine with a sentence. You want time travel? Invent the time machine. You want totally equal sex roles as in *Woman on the Edge of Time*? Invent the brooder. But even in realistic fiction, you can invent the world's biggest emerald or a new element or a formula for curing AIDS. The reader will not believe it if your protagonist survives in the last ten pages because of a sudden new cure for AIDS, but if that cure is carefully posited into the plot with convincing medical details and you are dealing with the effects on a country suddenly liberated from sexual fear, then posit away. The reader will accept your premises if the story is a good one and the characters are convincing.

There are many in-depth studies of plot, from those that analyze the elements of story structure in fairy tales and myths to the writing of screenplays. Many of them talk about the nature of The Quest, the search to satisfy a yearning or a need. They present the protagonist in the beginning of the story as existing in a kind of limbo, that is, knowingly or unknowingly, spiritually or materially, in an incomplete state in their lives. Perhaps, as with Oliver Single, in Le Carre's *Single & Single*, they are in hiding; or as with David Greene in *Storm Tide*, the protagonist finds himself with neither a career nor confidence in himself. In Richard Price's *Clockers*, being a drug dealer literally makes Strike, the protagonist, sick to his stomach. Suzanne, in *Three Women*, has yet to reconcile with her mother and her oldest daughter.

Sometimes this is called an Inciting Incident, or the Call to Action, or a Plot Point, but invariably some event shakes the protagonist out of their present state and sets them in motion to change. Oliver Single suddenly receives notice that five million pounds sterling have been deposited into his bank account; David Green meets a seductive older woman who recruits him to run for political office; Suzanne Blume's daughter loses her job and moves back in and Suzanne is presented a note in court: her mother has had a stroke.

The traditional three-act structure (set-up, confrontation, resolution) common to many plays and almost all commercial movies is the standard model used when talking about plot. Some books that discuss the finite number of recurring plots in literature even list films as examples. But here you have to use common sense. Novels are not screenplays. Novels do not have to conform to a rigid structure. Many novels are adapted for screenplays and rewritten to fit the classic three-act structure and in the process sometimes bear only a token resemblance to the book they were adapted from. Indeed, the most truly faithful novel-to-film adaptation I've ever seen is the British Granada Television version of Waugh's *Brideshead Revisited*. But of course this was a TV mini-series that ran about twelve hours rather than the standard Hollywood ninety-minute theatrical release.

Novels are about change over time, about memory and reflection, about characters and their most intimate thoughts. No less an important medium in our time, films are about characters changing through action. Novels depend on language to tell a story; films, visual imagery. Others have compared fiction and film far more knowledgably and in depth. We bring up the issue here only to make a point about confusing the two. Many writers who want to write fiction are more knowledgeable about film than they are about literature. They have seen hundreds of movies in their lives and have read only a fraction of that many novels. They are astonished that what works in film does not come across on the page.

Case in point, a novel we recently read in which an American diplomat meets and begins a relationship with a third world terrorist. The author was relying on a number of clichés to pull it off: that they were both good-looking, tall and thin; that they had good sex, the first time, every time; that the terrorist had been tortured and was therefore sympathetic; that the American diplomat was a lonely foreigner.

Every serious screenwriter will tell you that when they bring two characters together with the intention of showing them fall in love, it takes a lot more than two movie stars, some repartee, a series of facial close-ups, reaction shots and a love scene. But it is sometimes the case in writing fiction that we are seeing movies, and thinking in movie language, rather than trying to figure out how to show people making a real connection over time. We made a lot of suggestions to the writer. We asked her to think about describing them more fully: the small physical details that lovers notice, or the fascinating and sometimes even off-putting things that a person of one culture might notice in a person from another; the conversations but also the failures of language that would draw and repel two such lovers. Whereas it is true that a fine writer can say a lot with an image or a few perfectly chosen words of dialogue, fiction allows you the space to spread out and create an entire world, the world that in a film includes all those details provided by the actors and the designers, the costumers and location people. As a fiction writer you're not only writing the script, you're the entire company.

A woman approached me once in a workshop and said, somewhat confrontationally, "I'm a journalist. I don't write fiction because everything I need to say about a story I can say in a paragraph. Then I have nothing more to say." It turned out she did very much want to write fiction, but didn't understand that her five or six sentences were a mere outline of facts; that she was stopping short of the creation of her main character's yearnings, her history, family, friends, neighbors; where she lived, what went on in that town; the situations she looked forward to and those that she dreaded; all the details that would provide her protagonist with the interactions that constitute a believable and interesting life.

In the Afterword to the 20th Anniversary edition of her first novel, *Adult Education*, Annette Williams Jaffee writes about the genesis of an outline into a book:

> In the spring of 1979, two women named Becca and Ulli came to live with me. I had recently started working with the poet and novelist Maxine Kumin, who was teaching in the Creative Writing Department at Princeton University for the semester. I had sent her two very short stories – I couldn't write more than five or six pages at that time – and a letter saying: "I am a housewife trying to crawl out of her kitchen." Although I had wanted to be a writer most of my life, it was only six months before that I had begun writing with a certain seriousness I had never brought to

my work before, meaning I was actually writing, instead of just talking about it.

We were living on the lake then, in a split-level contemporary house and the bedroom which had previously housed a series of students who baby-sat in exchange for the room and an occasional meal – other people's difficult adolescent children was how I thought of them – was empty because my children, now 11 and 10, could finally stay home alone. I resigned from all my volunteer activities and gave myself five years to produce one publishable work – a short story, perhaps, in an obscure literary magazine

I had known Becca a long time, although I didn't know her name. For several years I wanted to write about this woman and the times she lived in; sometimes I called her Susan, sometimes I called her Sandra, but I could never get beyond a few flat first-person narrated pages. One of the stories I had sent Maxine was about a dancer named Becca. All of a sudden I knew the name of this woman! I knew she had been a dancer; I knew she had red hair. I knew everything about her. More importantly, I heard her voice – she talked to me all the time. The kitchen, my car, my bedroom became cluttered with scraps of paper with what Becca had to say to me. In fact, suddenly, everything anyone told me seemed to be about Becca. Her friend Ulli arrived differently. I had spent the academic year 1973–4 in Sweden, and Ulli became the culmination of that strange, mysterious, beautiful place for me.

I would meet with Maxine in her office every Monday for an hour. She would read what I brought her and I would watch her elegant face for signs of amusement, confusion, pleasure. She taught me that my stories were really outlines and needed to be filled out with details and dialogue. Sometimes she said they were finished as they were, sometimes she didn't have a clue of what to do to save them. After that hour, I would run indoors in the enormous skeletal university gymnasium – like Jonah in the belly of the whale, I thought – on a wonderful spongy track and pieces of fiction would float through my head. With my flushed face and all my pulses beating, it was like being in love.

By May, I had written about forty pages about Becca and Ulli and their husbands Gerry and John and the children, Christopher and Alexandra and Victoria. "Well," said Max at our last session together, "If you can write eighty more pages about these four characters, you will have a novella and maybe we can fix up some of these short stories and you will have a book." (A book!) More importantly, Max handed me on to Joyce Carol Oates for a tutorial the next fall.

"No," said Joyce, when I brought her my 75 pages in the fall. "It's not a novella, it's a short novel – about 180 pages – and here is how you begin."

Each Monday at three o'clock, I climbed the stairs at 185 Nassau Street to Joyce's office, usually stopping to chat with Richard Ford across the hall. He had published only one critically acclaimed novel at that point, so I wasn't too intimidated by him, and anyway, he had those lovely Southern manners. I assume he still has. Every week, I brought Joyce the next chapter I had written on the basis of her wise and gentle guidance. One week, I remember I was very distracted and didn't get much done and when Joyce questioned me, I said I was thinking about Thanksgiving and making a turkey. "Well, think about Becca making a turkey," she said. By April, I had written 180 pages. I remember how Joyce put the manuscript down on her desk and said very seriously, "You are now at a blessed point for any writer. You have a fine first draft of your novel. Treat it as if you will die and this is the only thing that you will leave behind."

In a spy story, the dramatic need of the main character may be to find the mole in the organization; or to bring an agent in from the cold; or to discover the secret formula. In a thriller, it might be to stop some catastrophe before it happens, such as stopping a madman before he sets off a bomb. Novelists sometimes use the device of the "ticking clock" to maximize suspense: that is, the problem must be solved in a certain amount of time or the catastrophe will occur. This is a common device on television and in films.

Thrillers and detective fiction, books about spies and cops, mysteries, are sometimes called plot-driven fiction, although, in the hands of a really good writer, all categories blur. In plot-driven fiction, the incidents that occur in the story mostly derive, not from the personalities of the characters, but from external forces out of the character's control and from incidents of chance.

In James Lee Burke's novel *Burning Angel*, a detective's house is trashed and two men are brutally murdered. These incidents are obstacles to the main character's dramatic need to solve a crime, but do not derive from his personality. Contrast this with a novel that is character-driven.

In James Leo Herlihy's *Midnight Cowboy*, the main character, Joe Buck, encounters many obstacles to his yearning to be truly needed by someone in the world. He's duped by a religious fanatic, fleeced by a con man and continually taken by the johns he's supposed to be taking, but all of this results from his personality. He's a country boy, totally out of his element in New York City; more, he's kind and dense and gullible.

In the chapter on creating character, we talk about the fact that the more you know about your characters, their histories, fears, their likes and their phobias, their habits, their weaknesses, the more there is to write about, the more trouble they'll get into, the more places they are likely to retreat to, the more problems they'll create for themselves. I've often heard people complain about thrillers they'd bought because the plot sounded fascinating, only to find that the book ultimately felt artificial. The characters seemed to be continuously facing obstacles that were created for them, like rides at an amusement park, rather than problems that, had the characters been given deeper personalities, they were likely to face in real life. The best plot-driven fiction, such as the novels of a writer like John Le Carré, use all the elements of character-driven fiction. A character's strengths and weaknesses, his or her history and longings, will determine many of the obstacles that he or she will face, and how he or she handles them as well. *Single & Single* is a globetrotting thriller about rogue London investment bankers entangled with the Russian mafia. There are as many explosions, shoot-outs and reversals as any *Mission Impossible* movie, but its protagonist, Oliver Single, is primarily driven by his complex and realistically drawn relationship with his con man of a father.

If you are writing what is sometimes termed character-driven fiction, stories based on the lives of people who are not in 'high concept' professions – bookstore owners, housewives and academics rather than four-star generals, homicide detectives and astronauts – you still want your reader to continue turning pages, and you would do well to pay attention to some of the basic elements of story telling usually employed by plot-driven fiction, such as difficult predicaments, reversals of fortune, and characters with conflicting needs.

This is not to say that the character is ever *only* about satisfying a need. Characters will meet many people and many things will happen to them. Time will pass and they'll make discoveries about life and maybe they'll have more than one great desire or maybe they won't even know what that is primary need is, but you the writer should have an idea about where they are headed and what they yearn for.

For instance, in Myla Goldberg's fine first novel, *Bee Season*, Eliza wants to enjoy her father Saul's love and attention, which has always been fixed on her brother; Saul wants a disciple, a progeny who will be brilliant in some way and share his passion for Kabbalah, Jewish mysticism. This is one of the novels in which it is characters getting what they want that gives them trouble.

However, the dramatic need is not always obvious. The character thinks she wants one thing, like money, when what she really wants is what she thinks money can buy: respect or freedom. Sometimes a character might think she wants sex, when what she really wants is human connection, an end to loneliness. If this is the case with your character, your story is even more interesting, because you're operating on more than one level: on the material level the quest for money or sex as well as on the deeper spiritual or psychological level the quest for love. Your character might even fail to get one thing she thinks she wants and get what she really needs. Or vice versa. She may get what she thinks she wants and find it does not satisfy her real or deeper needs.

People don't generally read novels or memoirs to observe characters breezing through life. Nobody gets a free ride. Life is about meeting challenges; solving problems. Characters change when they encounter conflict successfully or unsuccessfully. Just as there are some people who undergo the loss of a limb and continue forward with their lives with a deeper perspective, others become bitter and wallow in self-pity.

Some readers like to follow people like themselves, meeting, or knuckling under, to problems like their own. Others like to read about people who couldn't be less like themselves: professional athletes, gorilla researchers, double agents; the disabled, the dyslexic, the disinherited. It is true that a terrific writer, in command of her talent, can write an interesting novel about a woman who does little besides think and react to a day's occurrences, but you will often note that the day is very well chosen indeed and manages to bring up important issues and conflicts in that woman's life, as happens in Virginia Woolf's *Mrs. Dalloway*.

So what kinds of problems can your characters find themselves faced with? *Interior* conflicts are those problems or issues that arise from the traits inside a character's personality: guilt, greed, jealousy, envy, laziness, self-hatred, lack of confidence, the inability to make decisions, the habit of believing everything people tell you, the need to please authority. Your protagonist could harbor a terrible temper that always makes her blow up at the wrong people; your protagonist can suffer from the fear of being emotionally hurt that might make him run away from someone who loves him. On the other hand, a character can get into equal trouble from an obsessive need to be loved, which makes her attempt to seduce people and thus invite trouble. Interior conflicts in characters as well as the people we know tend to repeat and snowball. In *Midnight Cowboy*, Joe Buck's need to please people gets him suckered time after time until all the money he's saved is gone and he finds himself homeless.

Interpersonal conflicts are problems that arise between people and may or may not result from a character's own personality: a character's interaction with a sadistic boss; a really nasty neighbor; an abusive husband; a father-in-law who always tries to put her down. Rivals for a job or the love of the same person or divorced parents competing for a child's love: these are all examples of interpersonal conflict.

Interpersonal conflicts can happen as a result of pure chance: a band of Hell's Angels who appear in your character's rear-view mirror; a lover with whom she had the most exciting sex of her life twenty years ago moves in next door; a lonely widow falls into an affair with a man her son thinks is out to use up every dime she has. But it is in the interaction between the character's personality and history that sets up the response to the situation of conflict into which he or she is moving. For example, the son above feels terribly responsible for his mother because he was not there for her when his father was dying; or, he has been trying to fight his excessive closeness to her. Each produces a different course of action.

External conflicts: The natural world can create some impressive conflicts: A snowstorm made tough going for the Donner party. A stock market or plane crash may dampen a vacation. A large white whale plays havoc with the outcome of a whaling venture. All are disasters the characters had no part in creating, although usually the situation is set up to involve the personality of a leader or decision-maker: someone foolhardy or stubborn or driven, who insists on going forward in spite of danger or obstacles.

Things get even more interesting when external conflicts create interpersonal conflicts: An aging but very independent woman has a stroke and must then move into the home of the daughter whose life she never approved of; a bad snow storm causes a writer to drive off the road and be rescued by a sadistic, obsessed admirer. External conflicts can cause a person to act in a way that puts their personality to the test: A self-involved Jewish teenager must grow up very quickly when the Germans enter Paris and send her family to a concentration camp. Perhaps you're struggling with the issue of how to write about the lives of everyday working people. A prolonged labor strike can throw the citizens of any community into situations in which they meet conflicts on every level. This can happen in a mountain mining town; or rust belt Detroit; or downtown Los Angeles.

Most novels have their characters go through all kinds of combinations of conflicts while short stories tend to deal with more limited conflict, if any. Many short stories are slice-of-life narratives that may, like James Joyce's, offer an epiphany, a moment of insight. Or, like many *New Yorker* stories, they may simply give a quick view into someone's life.

Another way to look at plot is from the standpoint of what happens to the protagonist. The most elementary kind of plot consists of a *change of fortune* on the part of the protagonist, either a rise or fall. The personality, or deep inner character of the protagonist does not undergo any particular change either for good or ill and no interesting issues or moral or political or philosophical dimension are riding on what happens, although the story may be told to point a simple moral: money is the root of all evil, Thou shalt not kill, whatever. The story depends on suspense and perhaps surprise for its effect on us, or on a simple irony of fate.

When such a work rises above the ordinary, it is generally either because the milieu is tremendously well realized; or because one or more of the characters is strong enough so that we simply want to watch him or her in action. We do not want the character to change, but only to please us by doing what we expect of it, with variations. Arthur Conan Doyle's Sherlock Holmes stories are of this kind. However, I would point out that in the detective fiction of Dorothy Sayers, her protagonist Lord Peter Wimsey changes considerably.

There are other kinds of plots in which the protagonist does not change: those in which the main action is the suffering of the main character, often the heroine. Sometimes the emphasis as in Zola or Dickens is on the societal forces that have produced the misery; for instance war in Hemingway's *A Farewell to Arms*. Another case where the protagonist remains constant is the plot in which some particular strong character wreaks havoc and is punished. For all its richness of language and complexity of presentation and milieu, *Moby Dick* does not have a protagonist who changes. Ahab is as obsessed when we meet him as he is when he goes down lashed to the whale.

We have expressed the strong opinion that plot must issue from character. The better you know and the more completely you can enter your major characters, the surer you will be about their longings, what they want to do and what they will then try to do. Certainly the interactions and intersections and collisions of characters partially determine plot. However, the better you know your societal setting and the pressures of the time and place, social class and economic situation, the more you will know how these desires can or can not be translated into successful action.

Simply put, a doctor wants a mink coat. Her conflict would be largely internal. Is it right to own such a coat? Animals died for her to wear it. Is it appropriate to her life style, her social setting? But a coal miner in Wyoming wants a mink coat. That's a different story.

Successful action in this case is determined by scarcity, competition and consequence. What to eat for supper is not the stuff of high drama to a woman who sells commercial real estate in Manhattan, but to the displaced homemaker living as a bag lady on the street what she can buy in the supermarket to eat in her doorway – say the doorway of Abercrombie and Fitch in New York – is a fraught choice. She may not have another meal for two days. And for a mother in the Sudan trying to keep her child alive another day, eating or not eating is the stuff of life and death.

What I mean by what I know and don't know about the plot when I am writing a first draft I can show you with an example from *Gone to Soldiers*. I know that about a third of the way into the book, Jacqueline, a French Jewish teenager, and her mother have a serious fight, so that Jacqueline leaves home, not meaning to run away permanently, but keeping her away from home at a critical time – the night of the Grand Raffle when roughly twenty thousand Jews were picked up by the French police under instructions from the Gestapo. They were taken to a rink used for bicycle races in the winter, where they were held for eight days without food or water, including five thousand children, who died like flies. Then they were shipped to camps.

Now I have to remove Jacqueline from her mother's flat in Paris that weekend so that while her mother and younger sister are taken, she is not. I would like it, naturally, to be an absence not accidental or contrived – By the way, Mama, this Friday night I will sleep at my girlfriend's. So I figure with Jacqueline being nineteen in the hot summer of 1942 and out of college because she has been forced out for being Jewish, I will give her a boyfriend and she will at this time begin sleeping with him. That, discovered by her mother or in fact an honest answer on Jacqueline's part to such a question would get her into a fight where she would likely storm out of the flat. Such a fight could also make her feel quite guilty, which is useful to my plot. So Jacqueline has a boyfriend, who, to keep her out of danger that night, should not be Jewish. Who would be most indifferent at that time to the laws forbidding such association? One of the zealous, the zoot suiters of Paris, who defied the Nazis by wearing their hair long and greasy and listening to jazz and acting cool. Okay, now we have Jacqueline's boyfriend Henri emerging, and the plot begins to fill in.

When you must have characters quarrel, it is far better if the reasons for their quarrels do pertain (1) to the ongoing needs of the story; (2) to some revelation of character about one or both of the quarrelers; (3) to our understanding of the dynamics of the relationship; or (4) some point of the politics or economics or general situation of the characters of the society we ought to understand. In science fiction or in historical fiction, this latter reason may be particularly important.

Another common type of plot is that in which it is not so much the change in fortune or circumstance of the protagonist we are concerned with as a maturing (as in the classic Bildungsroman, i.e., *Portrait of the Artist as a Young Man* or the first three books of Doris Lessing's Martha Quest novels). Or in a variation, the plot is about a learning or changing experience, as in Conrad's *Lord Jim* or *Pinocchio*. But not all change is for the better. There are also tales of the degradation of character: for instance Conrad's *Heart of Darkness* or Faulkner's *Sanctuary*.

In some novels, the primary learning experience occurs not in the mind of any of the characters, but in what the reader is supposed to understand. These novels do not generally have a simple plot in the same sense that a novel fixed on a single or small group of protagonists may have. Dos Passos's *USA* trilogy; Doctorow's *Ragtime*; *Gone to Soldiers* are all examples of the genre. Only in the reader's mind will the final story assume its shape, for none of the characters can see what the reader sees or know more than their own stories. It is the pattern of the whole that is the "plot" and indeed such novels are usually roughly about some historical event: a war, a depression, a revolution, a particular moment in history.

Another type of plot is the revelation story: this is not the same as a mystery. It is not *who done it*, but *what the hell is going on?* A classic example is Shirley Jackson's much anthologized story, "The Lottery." The suspense lies in the protagonist and the reader figuring out the situation.

Coincidence is part of every plot. Little Red Riding Hood happens to meet the Wolf. He could have been off chasing a rabbit or snoozing. Most sizable predators sleep a fair amount. Ask your cat about that, a small predator but one who can explain much mammalian behavior to you, as can your dog. Your hero happens to win the lottery and get rich overnight. Two of your characters meet on plane after they have sworn never to speak again ten years before. A woman behind a fast food counter recognizes a face from the post office wall. Our lives are full of coincidences, and so is fiction. But a light hand is required. And it is far, far better to use coincidence to set up your plot than to use coincidence to resolve it.

That is, few readers will challenge you if your protagonist wins the lottery in an early chapter and the plot moves on from there, about the impact of sudden riches. But in the plot mentioned above where the coal miner wants a mink coat, if, in the end, she wins the lottery and gets it that way, we will feel cheated, manipulated. That is the difference between using coincidence to launch versus using coincidence to resolve. It is probable in general that we are able to accept complication from coincidence better than resolution from coincidence.

One problem with apprentice writing can be an over-elaboration of plot. It is something the writer keeps tripping over and that keeps tripping up the reader. Instead of going deeper into character, the writer keeps inventing new events, new schemes, new travels and twists of fate. Often the best plots are the simplest. Sometimes plots are borrowed and reinterpreted. A good story is always there for the retelling. World War II was a whopping good story and a lot of us have had a go at it over the years and a many more writers will come to it. King Arthur, Tristan and

Ysolde, Robin Hood, Bluebeard, Billy the Kid, Adam and Eve, King David, Helen of Troy, Faust: these names evoke basic stories that can be told again freshly in every generation. They can be made new again and again because they are rich in resonance and each writer finds something different in Merlin, in Guinevere, in Lancelot. The descent of the hero or heroine into the underworld to confront death in pursuit of knowledge, or some item, some person, some task, goes back to the story of Inanna's descent into the land of death as first told by the Sumerians, and we have been telling versions of it ever since. Such stories survive and are retold because they are capable of bearing great meaning, but that meaning changes over time. Arthur is one writer's fatuous fool, another's naive dreamer, another's failed schemer; for someone he represents what was left of Roman values, for another Celtic strength; for one he is Christianity's hero combating the ancient mother goddess religion; for another he is the last Druid king.

Plot is in many ways inseparable from questions of viewpoint. By looking seriously at Morgan le Fay in the cultural context of her times, by adopting her point of view, Marion Zimmer Bradley got a completely new angle on the Arthur stories. Many basic stories of our culture appear in the long run inexhaustible. Only some truly fresh approach and an apprehension of new and interesting values in the tale is needed.

There are certain plots always capable of reuse even though they lack that mythic dimension: for instance "The Pardoner's Tale" in Chaucer's *Canterbury Tales*, is also the plot of B. Traven's *The Treasure of the Sierra Madre*. Just as *Romeo and Juliet* serves as a model for *West Side Story*.

Occasionally a basic new plot emerges. Joanna Russ has identified a plot in the writings of a number of contemporary or relatively so (nineteenth century) women writers that could be called Rescue of the Daughter. Frequently the younger woman is not actually a daughter but is a daughter figure, one in whom a continuity of values or life can be expressed. She is stolen, lost or embedded in a hostile or dangerous situation. This is of course an old plot too, being your original Demeter and Persephone myth; but it has proved particularly prevalent in women's writing in the West in the last hundred or hundred-fifty years.

No plot contains within its outline any information on how serious it is, how meaningful, how lightweight. Take the basic mystery plot: a crime has been committed from which certain consequences are visible. Who done it? That's your basic formula mystery but also the plot of Sophocles' *Oedipus Rex*.

In the chapter in which we discuss viewpoint, we write about ironies that arise from flawed viewpoint or from multiple viewpoints. There are also ironies that are built into plots. The irony may be in the protagonist's sacrificing everything or working for years to attain something that when she or he gets it, destroys him or proves worthless. The irony may be in the character's trying to get rid of something that turns out to be necessary, precious, vital. These are ironies of plot, built into the basic story and developed through character but not issuing from it.

The most satisfying resolutions of plot tend to be those in which the ending feels "right" to us. However difficult that may be to describe, there is usually a correct reward or disaster or suspension awaiting the characters at the end of every story. This outcome should be one which issues either from the character of the protagonist or from the nature of the important relationships set up between the protagonist and important others, friends or enemies. In plot-driven fiction, the ending may be a stunning or exciting outcome to a course of action which should not be too easily foreseen but which doesn't come out of nowhere either.

Sometimes you may have to choose between more than one "right" ending (and indeed there are novels, like John Fowles's *The French Lieutenant's Woman*, that include more than one). We've all been disappointed at one time or another by the endings to some books we've otherwise liked. We may have felt that the author let us down, that they did not fully think through all the possible choices available to their characters, or they wrote in a happy ending where we expected disaster, let someone off the hook. Unlike today's commercial movies, in more complex novels, villains don't always get punished. The ending is your choice. However, in one of the most unsuccessful endings in a submission we received at the press, an ending that kept us from publishing the book, the writer began with an eerily created, quietly explosive rural town. A place in which people live in fear and keep their mouths, and curtains, shut. The main character, an army vet pushed to his limits, finally confronts the corrupt and omnipotent county sheriff. But by the end of the book the crooked cop had disappeared, as had the woman the protagonist had begun a relationship with, as well as her jealous, gun-toting half-brother. They simply dropped out of the last quarter of the book and were written off in a sentence at the end. If characters have become real to us and integral to the story, they cannot simply drop from sight or be quickly dismissed.

While all books are unique and it is difficult to theorize about the "right" or "satisfying" ending, you never want to create situations you can't fully imagine. If you can't bring yourself to write a fight scene, don't create a potential showdown between two violent characters that gets arbitrated off-stage by a kindly judge. All our experience would tell us that this is not what would happen. Therefore it doesn't strike us as "right" or "satisfying." When considering the ending to a plot, you don't by any means need to know it before you begin, but be prepared to finish what you start. The plot has to issue from what comes before it. The *deus ex machina* refers to the resolution of a drama in Greek theater by a god being lowered onto the stage to solve or resolve the situation. This would not work nowadays. (Unless, of course, as in *The Three Penny Opera* you are calling attention to it and attempting satire.) Your ending must arise from your story, rather than being tacked on or produced by an outside force.

The theory of story structure can be explored further. There are books that advertise themselves as analyzing the plots of every story ever written and contend that there are only a finite number of plots. There are books that go deeply into the structure of myths, list the common character types and map out sequences of action. There is never a danger in studying what others have learned, only in believing there is a formula for creating. In searching for a formula, rather than mastering the basic tools in your own way, you're basically renting a motel room, tacking paper to the wall and following a mechanical flow chart. Rather, allow yourself to engage in the mystery of the creative process.

Make 'Em Suffer – An Exercise for Creating a Plot

Some plots in their most basic form are quests. The protagonist wants something and spends the length of the story attempting to get it. When he or she does get it, we the readers feel a sense of satisfaction, because we watched someone work hard to achieve their goal. (Or maybe the protagonist fails to reach the goal – that's okay. You're the creator, you can do anything you want.)

Too many writers know the setting of their story, or the characters they want to write about, but fail to give their characters a material goal or an emotional yearning (or both!). The pursuit of this yearning sets your character into action.

Even fiction that is not about "action heroes" needs complication to set the characters in action.

In this exercise you are going to:

1. Create a protagonist (tell us their name and something about them).

2. Give that character a dramatic need, or an emotional yearning.

3. Create obstacles to achieving that need or satisfying that yearning.

Remember, we talked about:

1. Inner conflicts.

2. Interpersonal conflicts.

3. External conflicts.

And, if you can, figure out how (and if not why not) they achieve their goal.

Remember, too, sometimes we set out trying to find something we think we want and end up with something different altogether – and maybe not something tangible, but an emotional or intellectual understanding.

This exercise can be done in outline form. No complete sentences or graphic detail are necessary.

6

Personal Narrative Strategies

SOME YEARS AGO I HAD the following conversation with my mother: I was thinking about getting her some novels for her birthday and she said, No, she didn't think so. She didn't like fiction any more. Because I write fiction, there was an awkward moment, but when I pressed her as to why, she said, "Well, because, you know with novels it's. . . like somebody just made it all up."

Right. So I went out and got her a book of memoirs and she was thrilled. She loved it. So I asked, "What did you like about it?" She said, "Some true stories are like. . . I met this one and then I met that one, but this book, well, it's just like a novel."

What she meant was that the memoir presented her with a life that had a shape rather than a mere listing of events. It had a unifying idea and took the trouble to describe places and go deeply into characters, all the fundamentals necessary to lift a life story above the level of mere reporting. In short, all the things you find in a novel.

It seems to me we're a culture obsessed with personalities; from Walter Scott's "Personality Parade" to *People Magazine* to *Vanity Fair* movie star profiles to celebrity bios, we're nuts to know what goes on beneath the veneer of social discourse and that persona which we portray to others. Some of this curiosity is probably as low-minded as the tabloids themselves: we all like to see the high-and-mighty take a fall. Some of it is based on our own insecurity. We want to see how we're doing compared to the next person. If others suffer some of our same pain and frustration, then we're not such losers after all. But I think too, that we're all seeking the answer to a very fundamental question, What does it mean to be alive? In a world where we're running around sixteen hours a day, who has the time to put things in perspective? So we read about other people's lives in hopes of seeing a shape, a meaning, a direction in our own.

Depending on your tastes, you will select different lives to read about and obviously receive different kinds of insights. We'd like to think that the examined life of a saintly person would give us more moral or spiritual guidance than the memoirs of movie star, but on a very practical level, seeing the long term arc of someone who was admired by millions then drank himself to ruin just might be all the wisdom we need to turn our lives around.

The two questions we're most frequently asked in personal narrative workshops are these: How exactly do I organize the telling of a story as large as my entire life? On a more personal level, the question that seems to plague every writer contemplating a memoir: Is my story interesting enough to tell?

Let's take a look at three lives:

One was a World War II combat photographer. The second, a New York City homicide detective. The third, an eighty-year-old woman who lived with her cats in Maine. All three were writers. But, although the combat photographer arrived at Hitler's bunker the day after Hitler blew his brains out, then went on to witness the liberation of the concentration camps, his memoirs were returned by every publisher who saw his manuscript.

Although the homicide detective had worked deep undercover, infiltrating a fanatic terrorist group and rising through its ranks until he reached the leadership of the organization, he had been unable to place his memoir in every single venue he tried.

The old woman died at eighty-two-years-old. Her personal writings, largely about illness and solitude and things as mundane as her garden, her cats, and her friends – few of whom were famous – have been international best-sellers, translated into many languages and still in print long after her death.

As you may have guessed, her name was May Sarton. She was the author of some forty-eight books and as such took the trouble to learn what the two men who lived lives full of suspense and excitement did not: how to write about a situation and make it interesting to a reader.

So what makes interesting writing? I can tell you that in the case of the homicide detective, none of the characters he presented were well drawn. They were tall or short, bald or hirsute but he had failed to infuse his characters with life, to make them real by illustrating the nuances of their behavior, or describing what they longed for or contradictions that made them capable of bombing a building near a school at the same time as they were caring fathers to their children.

The life may be yours, but there are other people in it. If the story is going to hold a reader's attention, the most important of those people must be created with more depth than mere walk-ons.

I can tell you that in the writings of the combat photographer, he listed one fact after another. Montgomery crossed the Rhine on the night of March 23. The U.S. 17th Airborne landed in the enemy rear areas. The air column was two hours and thirty-two minutes long. Every fact was correct – and devastatingly dull. The writer was crushed; he didn't believe it. He was writing about World War II: the most fascinating conflict of the century. But there were no descriptions of the personal toll of battle on people's lives. The narrator's voice was a constant drone of facts, less compelling than a good newspaper article.

May Sarton's personal narratives, however, take mundane experiences and squeeze from them insights into the writer's own inner life and truths about the world. A subject does not have to be glamorous to be interesting, not if it is treated interestingly, that is, investigated by a curious mind for the human truths that the facts imply.

Let's take an example, in this case a kind of personal writing we all do, writing about a trip. Your diary might list mundane facts:

Stayed in a small hotel in the Marais. Paris is expensive. Ate in three restaurants then started buying take-out to bring it back to my room. Parisians basically tolerate you when you buy things but otherwise pretend you don't exist.

Your journal might choose certain facts more selectively:

I was shy about bringing food back up to my room and carried a large back pack at all times, enabling me to preserve my pride when undergoing the scrutiny of the consierge who never lifted his eyes from his newspaper but surely followed the smell of double creme goat cheese all the way up the elevator shaft. I did my shopping on the Rue Rambuteau, a winding grubby market street where the chefs of many small restaurants split their lists – one shopped for vegetables, the others poultry or fruit – before meeting at morning's end for coffee. I practiced my French outside every establishment, carefully constructing my sentences for the discriminating third assistant apprentice to the pastry chef who clucked at my stupidity while handing me change for a hundred franc note.

In a memoir, however, we might squeeze the situation in order to reach that place where the personal touches upon universal experience:

The large clock at the Gare de l'Est read five-forty; exactly ten minutes until departure.

"S'il vous plaît, monsieur," I said again, as I had after every fractured sentence cobbled from my phrase book. More slowly this time: "Deux second échelon ticquet à Limoge, non fumant?"

Through the tarnished brass bars of the cage, the ticket seller appraised my worth. Foreign. Male. Middle class. No one who knew his name or his superior or whose complaint would mean a thing. Nothing I was or had ever been, no accomplishment in my life, no feigned kindness on my part, not even my evident need moved him. I watched the large hands of the station clock move. Five minutes to departure.

Clumsily, I repeated myself.

He sighed. "Je ne peux pas vous comprendre, Monsieur."

What did he not understand? What was I saying incorrectly? We had reservations for a rental car in Limoge. A hotel was booked and paid. It was too late to find a room in Paris for the night and we hadn't an extra franc to spend. We had to make this train.

The woman in line behind me cursed. The man behind her shouted something I did not need to have translated.

All our belongings, our suitcases, lay at our feet. The official looked through me, the smudge of sweat on my forehead, the reek of my nervous breath. "Suivant!" he signaled the woman behind me.

I blocked her path and pressed my face to the cage. "Can you understand English?" I tried one last time. "Can't you speak English with me?"

I saw the first hint of a smile. "Naturellement," he said. Of course he could speak English. "Mais pas à Paris." But not in Paris.

In the smug set of his mouth I recognized the disdain I myself had shown the gypsies who surrounded me in the train station in Prague, an old beggar in Earl's Court. I knew that petty Parisian bureaucrat would forever alter the way I treated a stranger in need.

In at least one way, autobiography is the opposite of biography. Autobiographers know everything; biographers never know enough. Biographers have to research a life for many years to figure out what to put in; *you* have to concentrate on what to leave out. You can't possibly tell us everything about yourself, so you need a narrative strategy.

The plot of a novel might involve a character with a longing, a need – say, to find someone who ran away with his lover; or an emotional need – to come to terms with her lack of education, to accept herself. The problem of satisfying this longing might be the arc of the action of the book, commonly called the plot. The need can't be satisfied too easily, of course. The reader wants to observe the character over the course of time, wants to watch her interact with others and make decisions in difficult situations. So the writer creates obstacles that force the character into action.

Braided Lives is a novel about a young woman from a working-class family in Detroit who desperately wants to be a writer in spite of the fact that she has no financial or emotional support from her family and faces the dead end life of many poor young women in the Midwest of the 1950's. An autobiographical novel was Marge Piercy's strategy for telling her story.

If you are shy about the effect of your story on other people, fiction may afford you the distance you need in order to discuss your life. Obviously, if you label your piece fiction, the reader is never sure what is true and what is not. But even more importantly, you the writer are encouraged not to stick to the absolute facts as they happened, but to create variations on the theme that was your experience.

The most apparent strategy is to change the names and the places. Once you do even this much, you find that strange characters tend to join

89

the party. For example, if you shift your family drama from Ocean Parkway in Brooklyn to an ocean liner in the mid-Atlantic, you need a captain and a crew and other passengers to make the voyage real. Suddenly there are people around who had nothing to do with your family. Now each character may be true to the role they played in the family – that is, the bitter and demanding old-world family matriarch or the youngest son who steals – but the scenes in which they interact might be quite different. A storm at sea could replace the fire that gutted your third floor apartment. People are true to character no matter what the disaster; indeed, no matter what the time period or setting.

Some writers go back in time to tell their stories, place their characters in historical situations, while remaining true to their own experience. Other writers choose science fiction. Their characters live on distant solar systems, three hundred years in the future. But what concerns those characters three centuries from now may very well be a father and son who cannot communicate; or a daughter troubled by her mother's addiction; or a woman who is in love with her sister's husband. It is naive to imagine that people in the past were free of the complications we suffer through today and overly optimistic to think that people in the future will face no interpersonal problems.

Piri Thomas, the author of *Seven Long Times,* chose to write about his life through a series of short stories set in prison. Toni Morrison says that her literary heritage is her autobiography and that through her novels she is imagining the interior lives of her ancestors, slaves in the southern United States. She says, "These people are my access to me. They are my entrance into my own interior life."

No matter which of the narrative strategies you try out or decide to pursue, you still have the problem of looking over your life and deciding what to put in and what – the bulk of daily life – to leave out. Consider that many writers, like Lillian Hellman and May Sarton, have produced a number of books about their lives, each focusing on a particular theme, a particular era, a particular important other or crisis. There are probably as many narrative strategies as there are writers, but a number of them emerge time after time. An obvious one is to start from childhood and work toward the present in chronological order. Some people's childhoods make fascinating reading; they had famous and powerful relatives (Gore Vidal), or they lived through extraordinary times (J.G. Ballard in

Empire of the Sun's World War II Shanghai) or they themselves (Simone de Beauvoir) had precocious insights.

Another strategy is to start with a particularly interesting time in the near present, as Mark Matousek did in his memoir *Sex, Death, Enlightenment*, and go back to childhood to dramatize the various forces that shaped his personality. Then he resumes going forward to the present. *Sex, Death, Enlightenment* is a spiritual journey, yet another narrative strategy. The arc of action in the book is the author's search for meaning in his life.

Kingsley Amis tells the story of his life through remembrances of people he has met; Lillian Hellman does the same. In both cases the author's friends and enemies are the jumping off points of the piece, allowing the author to riff about the politics and the mores of the times they lived in, their ideas about everything from sex to art, but the actual subject is the author because we're in their view point, seeing and experiencing every encounter through their unique sensibilities.

Memoirs, as opposed to full-fledged autobiographies, often shed light on certain aspects of the writer's life rather than reconstructing their days on earth from start to finish. Writing about subjects that have touched your life, such as people you have known, or cats, or your years in school, or music, or each of your lovers, or every car you ever owned or one particular house you lived in, can be the scaffolding you can build your narrative strategy upon. Remember, you are writing about yourself and your thoughts and feelings and emotions as they relate to these touchstones. You can go back and forth in time and memory, dip into childhood or the present for a few paragraphs or pages as your story dictates.

Now you may think you know everything there is know about your life but it's not always clear exactly what your story is, where you fit into it and what you are trying to tell the reader.

The *New York Times* columnist and PBS Mystery host Russell Baker told great stories about his huge family and was encouraged by his editor to write something they both referred to vaguely as "the growing up book." In a speech at the New York Public Library in 1986 (reprinted in *Inventing the Truth: The Art and Craft of Memoir*, edited by William Zinsser) Baker said that he put it off for years until he decided, in the 1960's, that he needed to communicate to his children some sense of the pride and dignity of their family. Some years later, his mother was stricken ill and he decided in due respect to her to write about the times he and his mother went through together. Being a reporter, he packed his tape recorder and interviewed his vast array of relatives and transcribed the interviews and came up with a four-hundred-fifty page manuscript about all the hard but wonderful times of family generations gone by. He sent the manuscript to his editor and waited for a response. And waited. And waited. All experienced writers know that an agent's (or editor's) enthusiasm is inversely proportional to the amount of time they take to read your manuscript and get back to you. Overnight: they love it big time. Weeks: you're in for trouble. When no response came, he knew something was wrong. When he reread the book, he realized that although this was to be a story about a boy and his mother, known as a remarkable but tough-minded lady, he had dutifully recorded all his relatives' interviews but had left himself and his mother out of the book. It was nothing but journalism, an accurate but not very compelling sketch of the Great Depression.

Baker decided he had to delve deeper. He had access to his mother's keepsakes, specifically her trunk. Inside it he discovered several interesting things. One was a cache of love letters between his mother and a man he had never realized she cared for; the other was her marriage certificate, which proved that Russell Baker was a love child, conceived out of wedlock. This discovery cleared up a lot of things for him, mysteries about his mother that he never understood, such as the animosity between her and his father's mother. Beforehand, this relationship had been incomprehensible. Now on the one hand, he feared that to mention these very personal discoveries in his book would be "airing dirty linen" and exploiting his mother's past for commercial purposes. On the other, he felt if he wanted to honor his mother's life, he had to be truthful. He had to show her as a person who acted as she did for good reason. So he decided to rewrite the book concentrating on just a piece of his life, a story line he referred to as the tension between a mother and son. His strategy in this book was to cast light on one corner of his life, albeit a significant one. He left out a great deal of material that failed to contribute to that story – which amounted to most of that original four-hundred-fifty-page manuscript.

Any memoir or autobiography is a way of investigating the substance of your own life or a segment of it, a theme running through it. Others will sometimes come to your writing asking the same questions as you yourself must ask when you are writing: what are the full implications, the essence of my experiences. Perhaps you are writing for the next generation. Perhaps you are writing lest you or others forget something important. Perhaps you are just trying to make sense of what you have done and what has been done to you. No matter what your intention, you just can't simply record what happened. You have to shape and examine it.

You can think of the facts as vessels – empty until you fill them with meaning and imagination. One day at a family gathering, a boy falls in the river. That's a fact. But what does it mean until I tell you that his father, a cold and secretive man, bitter about his own difficult childhood in the slums of a Midwestern city, famously afraid of deep water, dives in to save him. Until I recount the shame the boy feels at causing his father to flail awkwardly in front of the relatives to stay afloat; and the boy's guilt, at the same moment he is struggling for air, that he has caused his father to ruin his one good suit. What is a mere fact in light of the boy's realization, for the first time in his life, of his inscrutable father's deep love for him. In retelling the facts, in recounting what the facts imply, they may resemble a new situation. The experience won't be exactly like the one you lived through, but more intense. The incident may have been over in sixty seconds while it may take you years to figure out its implications; days or months to write it. As we have remarked earlier, sometimes when you shape your own experience whether in personal narrative or in fiction, you lose the memory as it happened. The artistic reconstruction of the event replaces what actually happened on that day or in that year, because it is more shaped, more vivid, more meaningful. You create a small world of your own with meaning that reaches out to others. If you want people to make the effort to read about that world, you have a responsibility to your reader. You must make your characters real and convincing and multi-dimensional. Your descriptions should make your physical details vivid. Mere reportage and statistics, however faithful to the truth, do not make interesting reading.

When you search out your narrative strategies, you might choose a subject, rather than your entire life, that you can infuse with your unique language and intelligence. M. F. K. Fisher used food. Willie Morris, his dog Skip.

Don't worry if you don't think you have an interesting life. Senators and generals, trial lawyers and movie stars, for all the glamour in their lives, are constantly writing less than interesting books about them. V.S. Pritchett was right on the money when he said, "It's all in the writing. You get no credit for living."

The Exercise: the Parallel Universe

Think of an incident in your own life. It can be an argument, or an erotic experience, or your first music recital; some memorable incident. The best incidents for this exercise carry some emotional weight: happiness or misery, fear, nervousness, embarrassment. (If it's been an incident you've been reluctant to tackle in your writing, so much the better.)

You are going to write about that incident. You are the main character in that story. But... you are going to disguise things in a big way.

Here are some suggestions (choose one or more):

1. Write in the third person.

2. Pick a main character that is not you.

3. Change the place the incident occurred.

4. Change the time period (make it happen in the past or the future).

5. Change the sex of the character.

Naturally, you'll have to make adjustments. If your incident concerns a crush you had on the captain of the ice hockey team and you decide to set your piece in Barcelona instead of Minnesota, the object of your affections will also have to change to accommodate the new surroundings (maybe captain of the soccer team? maybe a matador?).

Your aim is to be *true to your emotions* and *your version of the incident* but to distance yourself from it, disguise it so that:

1. The average reader of the piece would not see you in it but feel what you felt and,

2. Perhaps more importantly, you can write your story without worrying about whether someone will see you in it or whether you are betraying other people.

7

Choosing and Manipulating Viewpoint

I N DISCUSSING CHARACTERIZATION, we looked at the chemistry involved in characters in fiction – our attraction to them, repulsion from them. Often we respond to them as we would real people or sometimes as we would "selves" we put on. We may even imitate a particular character we identify with. There are three basic strategies for dealing with that chemistry.

In the first case, you want the reader to keep an emotional distance from the characters, as in Brecht's *Threepenny Novel,* as in the work of Sol Yurick and in Doctorow's *Ragtime* and *Loon Lake.* You intentionally and repeatedly distance the reader from the characters by the tone, by the placement of the vision, by a maintained coldness, by certain comic effects, by interposing a very strong voice between character and reader, or by adapting an omniscient point of view well above all the characters, in order to make them seem more like robots or ants and less like people we might know.

The second strategy for viewpoint occurs when you want the reader to identify with one character strongly. (Doris Lessing's Martha Quest series, Charlotte Brontë's *Jane Eyre*, Margaret Atwood's *Surfacing*, Barbara Kingsolver's *The Bean Trees*.) They will go through your narrative looking out through the eyes of that particular person and only that person.

In the third case, you give the reader a choice of characters to identify with, at least two and perhaps several to choose among. In Myla Goldberg's *Bee Season,* viewpoints alternate between the father, the mother, the younger sister and the older brother. In the recent three-generational novel *Living To Tell,* by Antonia Nelson, the viewpoint moves from family member to family member.

I have usually tried to get readers to identify with my characters. Why encourage it? When we identify with fictional characters, they offer us the opportunity to slip into someone else's skin: a woman, a man, an African-American teacher, a Chicano entrepreneur, a Native American farmer, a Norwegian dock worker, a Japanese physicist, a politician in Kenya, a midwife in Texas, a Neanderthal woman, a sled dog, a purple arthropod from Deneb 4. When we can empathize with others, we can less easily reject the alien or what we perceive as the alien, because it truly becomes less alien to us. We enter another consciousness and experience life in somebody else's shoes or boots or moccasins or ballet slippers. Like the life in dreams, it is not real but it can alter our perceptions, change what we think and do.

We imitate fictional characters. How many men still play Hemingway who played his own characters? Byron's heroes in his narrative poems inflamed a generation of young men and sometimes young women who wanted to play those parts too. Characters in the novels of the Beats have reemerged to inspire another generation of young people in khakis, black leather and t-shirts not to mention Bukowski's nouveau-chic barflies. An acquaintance of mine in college had an affair with an instructor based on the fact that both of them passionately wanted to live in a Henry James novel, in the late style.

Another important tactical choice has to do with how much you want the reader to trust your viewpoint character's observations and reactions. This is quite distinct from whether or not we identify with a character. The power of the sense of dramatic irony often rests in identifying with a character who does not perceive what is bearing down on her or him, while you see and feel the approaching shock wave. Some of the best comic effects can come from our perceiving how a character is "doing it again" – once again digging a grave with his tongue, lying, exaggerating, boasting, whatever is his prevailing vice.

There are varying ways of using a viewpoint character, depending on how much of what the character tells us we are to accept as the truth.

You may choose a viewpoint character who is pretty much transparent in that respect. i.e., you want us to see what they see and believe what they believe, to know neither more or less. Conrad's narratives are like this. So is Nick Carraway in F. Scott Fitzgerald's *The Great Gatsby*. Nick is everybody's friend, and as he comes to understand the characters, so do we.

You may choose a viewpoint character who knows less than we do. An example might be a child's viewpoint. We also might know more than any one character in a multiple viewpoint novel. We accept that the person is honest and perceptive, but we know things they don't yet know. A certain amount of energy can be generated by our sense of how a character's naiveté or ignorance or mistaken beliefs may be about to wound or destroy her or him, or wreak havoc on others. The hopefulness of the narrator's voice in *The Diary of Anne Frank*, and her continuing discovery of life is especially moving given what we readers knew to be her fate.

You may choose a viewpoint character who is a flawed, a distorting lens. We learn as the story proceeds to disregard much of what that character believes, as in John Fowles's *The French Lieutenant's Woman* or his *The Collector* or Mark Twain's *A Connecticut Yankee in King Arthur's Court*. The character may even be lying to us, and as in real life, we have to try to separate the reality from the obfuscation.

In the first type – the transparent narrator – you are expected to accept pretty much the judgment of the viewpoint character whether first or third person. In the second type, where each viewpoint character knows only part of the picture, you supplement what each knows with knowledge you the reader have learned elsewhere. In the third type – the mistaken or duplicitous narrator – you the reader are required to exercise caution and your own judgment. The character may be lying or may be merely fooled or wrongheaded, but you are on your own to figure out the truth. Humbert Humbert in Vladimir Nabokov's *Lolita* warns us straight-away to beware of a murderer with an fancy prose style.

Another tactical choice is whether to tell a story from a single viewpoint, a multiple viewpoint or omniscient viewpoint – or from the viewpoint of a character who in essence sounds as if he or she is omniscient, because that narrator knows how the story comes out and what led up to that denouement. For instance, the recent novel *The Family Orchard* by Nomi Eve begins with a section called "I Tell," in which a narrator addresses her husband and talks about how the story begins and suggests she knows things she has not told him, some inside or hidden knowledge. The true omniscient narrator who is above the story was most common in nineteenth-century fiction and is common in potboilers today, but far rarer in literary fiction. This narrator knows what everybody is thinking and feeling, what everybody is doing – the narrator knows everything the author knows. With this kind of omniscience, withholding information from the reader, such as who done it or an important character's shady past, is not an option.

Every time you switch viewpoints, you gain information and dramatic irony and new perspectives, but you lose momentum. You may lose the reader. It is a very important choice you make.

What you need to do before you begin any piece of fiction, whether short story or novel, is to figure out exactly where – from whose viewpoint – the story must be told. What must the reader see and know? In whose head are we going to be situated? Or is it a tale without a visible teller? If it is a tale told by someone – then to whom? to what end? And then the question returns, is that someone an idiot, a wise woman, a liar? Once again, is that viewpoint transparent or cracked?

A related tactical question is how close in to what you perceive as the center of the story do you want locate your viewpoint? Let us say we are writing the story of a divorce. The husband's story is one, the wife's another, and alternating them creates an extremely different texture. The viewpoint of a friend who can comment is quite different again. So is the viewpoint of the other woman or the other man, or someone who wishes to be one or the other. In every case, a very different story or novel will be the result of whose story you choose to tell, and whether you wish to present that story – let us say the wife's story is our center – according to how she herself sees it or according to how someone who wishes her ill or well, or who is truly neutral in the divorce, may see it. All of those are a priori choices, wisely made before you begin to write.

However, one thing you learn is that when a story or a novel is going poorly, sometimes it is time to stop and ask these questions again. It may be that the story is being told from the wrong viewpoint, or that another is needed to supplement the one being used, or a different standpoint may be required altogether. You may want to add a viewpoint or viewpoints, or simply change the head you are living in to tell the story. The voice of Mary, the homeless woman in *The Longings of Women*, was originally written in the first person viewpoint and in second draft changed, to much better effect, to third person.

If you are telling a complex social or political story, or perhaps the story of a very large family over the generations, you may well need multiple viewpoints. But each time you go into a new person's head, remember what you are losing. You take a chance of confusing the reader. You lose momentum. You lose any identification and rapport so far built up. You have to make this judgment freshly for each additional character you conceive of entering. But if you need to have the reader see your fictional world from multiple angles, you may choose to use multiple viewpoints. I often do that – certainly not always, but better than half the time – because while I encourage identification, I want the reader to arrive at their own truth, rather than buying the opinion of any one of the characters.

Remember that it is equally important to decide when you are using multiple viewpoint, whose life you want to enter because you want the reader to know what that person knows, and whose life you do not want the reader to see from within, because of destroying suspense. For instance, when the chief suspense element in your plot is who did something – whether it was stabbing the body in the library with a sharpened back scratcher, or writing a poison pen letter that destroys a friendship – if you enter the life of the person who did the act in question, you owe it to the reader to let her or him know what you know and what that character knows. Not all suspense resides in who did what. A great deal comes from such diverse questions as: will they realize they're in love, will they learn what X knows, will they get it together, will they succeed or fail, will she finally leave the jerk, will he realize she's using him, will he get the money in time, will she agree to the operation. Not only mysteries or adventure stories make use of suspense. Suspense is one of your basic seductions in getting the reader to read and keep on reading.

Similarly, if you use omniscient viewpoint, you may gain a kind of strong narrative voice otherwise available only in first person or with a narrator who lends a definite flavor to the story with their voice. You can go anyplace you feel like and witness anything convenient to your story.

But you can't withhold information from the reader, for you are in fact omniscient. That is why omniscience is seldom a good device in a mystery. Omniscience means you the writer are situated well above all the characters and can tell us what every one of them is thinking as well as doing. This may happen in telling or it may happen from simply shifting viewpoints constantly, as you find convenient.

Third person is the style of narration most commonly used:

He strolled down the causeway with his shoes in his hand.

Or:

Dorothy stood at the head of the stairs listening to the conversation below, straining for her own name.

Second person is a trifle cutesy, used at best for something short.

You walk down the street, you turn and look behind you. You stop at the corner for a light and you remember that guy at the party last night, the one with the throaty voice and the great grin.

First person is often used in autobiographical fiction but third person can be employed to create a distance from the actual teller of the story, a fictional self. There are times it has even been used in personal narrative. In *The Armies of the Night,* Norman Miler created a third person character named Norman Mailer. Writing about himself in the third person gave him some distance and a sort of dry perspective, enabling him to watch himself from above and comment on his own thoughts and behavior.

In Pam Houston's collection *Cowboys Are My Weakness,* she uses the second person in a number of stories. In "How to Talk to a Hunter" it has the effect of inclusion, as if to say, "You all know what it's like to be with a guy like this." There are fewer novels that use second person. In Jay McInerney's *Story of My Life* it is used by the narrator, Allison Poole, an 80's big city party girl, and creates the illusion of the way a lost young woman might speak.

Second person can work, but it can also feel like someone buttonholing you and insisting you agree with whatever line they are putting out. It's like sitting next to a stranger in a bar who keeps asking, "You know what I mean? You know what I'm saying?" until you wonder if you really do.

First person is used frequently in fiction and is the most common form used in the personal narrative. First person brings with it the identification available from the colloquial speaking voice.

From *Look At Me* by Lauren Porosoff Mitchell:

> I stood at the buffet where I could meet just about anybody at the party, except the anorexic of course. My half-glass of wine from the cash bar clutched in my hand, I was hoping to get lucky or even semi-lucky, someone to talk to, to avoid resembling a potted plant.

That direct first person invites you in and whispers in your ear and can be used for direct address, exhortation, special pleading and everything in between. It has ultimate freedom because it has the spontaneity of the speaking voice, and it can have that intimacy. You can freely move around in space and time, editorialize and give or withhold information and insight as someone does in conversation. However, its vices are as flagrant as its virtues. It has a tendency toward talkiness if not kept on a tight hold and can lead to an easy filling up of the page with nothing in particular, the long-windedness that destroys concentration and reader interest. Certain scenes are more difficult in first person. Sex scenes take careful handling.

A strong first person can seduce the reader, or can put her or him off, for if the reader takes a dislike to your character's voice, the book may go unread. I recently began reading a manuscript where the narrator was a domestic whose voice was so whiny and irritating I could not finish the story. The question of matching voice to character is another tactical decision. A bad first person can feel like someone shouting in your ear, and that can be tiresome indeed.

Some authors write the whole book in one voice. Others switch voices when they switch viewpoints. It is a matter of preference. Again, there are advantages to staying with one voice, in the unifying flavor it gives to a novel. There are advantages to switching voices if you switch viewpoints, for you have then one more device for characterization, and the reader will pick up quickly which head you are in if the voice is markedly different.

Finding a voice can be a challenge. Oftentimes I find that if I know my character well, I have my voice. It comes from within the character and sounds like her, as Connie's voice goes throughout *Woman on the Edge of Time* in the third person narration that never leaves her viewpoint until the documents at the end from the hospital staff.

However, with ten viewpoint characters in *Gone to Soldiers*, I paid attention to differentiating their voices. When I finished second draft, I took the book completely apart and wrote the third draft as ten separate novels, so that each character's story would be consistent in language, style, the minor characters, the time line, the feel of that character's world, their ambiance. Then in fourth draft I put it all back together. Many novels only take four drafts. *Gone to Soldiers* took six, and parts of it went above twenty.

Often when a writer of fiction is starting out, all the fuss about viewpoint seems overly technical and he or she may think, I'll just tell the story. But it doesn't work that way. Whose story are you telling? One of the standard exercises to understand viewpoint is to write the same scene from the point of view of two antagonistic characters: say a mother or father trying to discourage a son or daughter from continuing in a romantic relationship; and then from the standpoint of the son or daughter; then from the viewpoint of the lover being argued about. You may find your story is very, very different depending in whose head you situate yourself and therefore your reader. But the exercise works no matter what situation involving a clash of wills that you use.

When you are writing personal narrative, viewpoint may not be as pressing a consideration, but there are still aspects to consider. Most personal narratives are told in the first person, but there are many autobiographical novels and short pieces in which the author decides to put some distance between her or himself and the story. Sometimes you may begin in the first person and find that it somehow inhibits you when you are telling your own story. You may decide to take another pass at the material by changing the voice to third person. This is a common way to solve the problem of narratives that feel too private for the author to tell us or that might put the reader off by seeming too intimate. The writer may worry that the story told by "I" will seem too full of special pleading or self-pity or self-congratulation. The writer may feel safer, more comfortable with third person.

Sometimes a writer creates an alter ego and writes books in that alternate voice that sees the world through a perspective similar to their own. The short-story writer Grace Paley usually employs the witty and wise voice of a working class New York mother named Faith. Philip Roth has written several books through the voice of a New York Jewish writer who became rich and infamous through a scandalous, semi-autobiographical best-seller. Creating an alter ego for yourself is a way to blend reality and imagination and have fun doing it. You can always point to your character and insist, "I didn't say that. He did."

There is no right or wrong way to choose and establish viewpoint in personal narrative any more than there is in fiction. If one approach doesn't feel comfortable and it clenches you up to work that way, try another approach. Do what works for you.

Some writers choose to tell their own story in the form of fiction, as we have remarked before, in order to create a greater measure of distance between the story and themselves, and perhaps in order to gain freedom to explore potentially volatile, painful and shameful materials. Obviously if you label your piece "fiction," the reader can never be sure what's true and what's not. Perhaps more importantly, you, the writer, are not forced to stay with the facts but are free to invent scenarios that are emotionally true, what should have happened, what almost happened, what you dreamed happened. It surprises some people that the Chinese restaurant scene in Ira Wood's *The Kitchen Man*, never actually happened. For years his mother asked him, "Did we ever go out for Chinese food with you and Marge?" Not once, to a Chinese or any other kind of restaurant. But even to the participants, it feels like it happened because all the emotions and characterizations ring true. That greater freedom may empower you or dismay you. Experiment. Becoming conscious of the various options that are open to you in your writing is one of the biggest gifts you take away from any workshop, course or how-to book.

Some Exercises:

Take a simple story such as Little Red Riding Hood and reverse the usual point of view, that of the little girl. Write the story from the point of view of the wolf. YOU are the wolf. Get inside the wolf. How does the world look to him? Remember, he is the hero of his own story. Make at least a start on seeing the world through wolf eyes.

Other suggestions: the Three Bears from the point of view of the littlest bear; Snow White from the point of view of the Queen; Rapunzel from the viewpoint of the witch; Rumpelstiltskin from the point of view of the dwarf. Remember that "villains" are heroes to themselves, and the center of the story and the center of sympathy.

Another Exercise:

Take any scene from your own life and write it, not from your point of view, but from that of another person involved in the situation – perhaps someone antagonistic to you or in disagreement with you. It should prove interesting.

8

Descriptions

DESCRIPTIONS ARE PLACES where writers feeling their oats often let themselves go and readers nod off, put down the book or at their kindest, skip. No description should be skippable, but every one should be functional. If you describe something, make it work. In a work of fiction, a description might have a function in the plot. Perhaps you plan to use that jaunty red dingy in Chapter Four.

In both fiction and memoir, a description may suggest character, as in describing someone's bedroom or their apartment or their clothing. It may set a mood. It may place your characters in the socioeconomic spectrum.

From *Small Changes*:

Beth was looking in the mirror of her mother's vanity. The mirror had wings that opened and shut. When she was little she used to like to pull them together around her into a cave of mirrors with only a slit of light. It isn't me, isn't me. Well, who else would it be, stupid? Isn't anyone except Bride; a dress wearing a girl.

Beth could not help seeing herself in the mirror; could never call up a glamorous image as her younger sister Nancy could. Nancy was sulking in the bathroom because her best friend Trudy had called her a dishwater blond. Like Beth, Nancy had naturally curly, almost kinky light brown hair. They were the little ones in the family. Just yesterday she had picked off the floor a piece of paper with gum stuck in it written in Nancy's fancy new backhand: *Nancy Phail is a petite vivacious blond with loads of personality.* Nancy could look in the same mirror and see faces from those teenage magazines she brooded over. But Beth saw Beth lost in a vast dress. She felt like a wedding cake: they would come and slice her and take her home in white boxes to sleep on under their pillows.

With their married sister Marie's help, Nancy had written a description for the paper and mailed it in, though they never printed that except for people like, oh, executives' daughters from the G.E. plant where her father worked at the gate. "Schiffli embroidery and ribbons dip softly over an organza skirt and bodice, with sheer daintily puffed sleeves," Nancy had written. "The train comes away." That meant the thing that dragged could be taken off, with a little timely help.

Description may give us information about the society, if it is one exotic to us.

From *City of Darkness, City of Light*:

He went to Versailles with Turgot reluctantly. None of his talents counted. No one cared about mathematics, social theory or philosophy. They treated him the way people behaved when served the new and nutritious vegetable, potatoes, earth apples. They stared at the objects on their plate and toyed with them. So the bored and haughty courtiers stared at him, an earth apple if they had ever seen one, and attempted to toy with him. Ladies of middle rank flirted. He could not flirt back. He hardly found them of the same species. A woman who took six hours to dress, whose hair loomed a foot over her head, who was painted bright gold with red splashes and artificial moles, who reeked of violets and attar of roses and was packed into a dress that stood out three feet on either side of her, inspired him with nothing but a kind of contemptuous fear. All the courtiers were ranked by absurd roles (the countess who handed the Queen's first lady of the bedchamber the royal petticoat; the comte who stood on the King's left as his shirt was buttoned) and their privileges, both formal (who could sit on a stool in the royal presence and who must stand) and informal (the marquis the Queen danced with last night; the lady she smiled at; who had made the King giggle).

Versailles was an unnecessary city, built on ostentation as if on sand. It was larger in land than all of Paris and enclosed by walls. The streets were lined with the houses of officials whose functions were frivolous, and storehouses that held too much of everything. One building housed two hundred seventeen royal coaches. In Turgot's coach as they made their way through the crowded street, they passed the residences of men who cleaned the palace fountains, men who helped the king to hunt birds, who tended his packs of dogs, ten men in charge of crows, six of blackbirds. Scores of almoners, chaplains, confessors, clerics, choristers, the hundreds employed in the royal chapel or in providing sacred or profane music, clustered around the churches. Hairdressers alighted from carriages with the air of great generals, as heavily floured as bakers. The amount of flour consumed in a day in Versailles to powder the court's hair could feed Paris.

Description may make a satiric point.
From *The Kitchen Man*:

Wellfleet.

The summer town where a piece is not a nubile teenager or a triangle of boardwalk pizza but an essay in the *New Yorker*. The town where 1.4 members of every family has an agent, where psychiatrists block the narrow aisles of the local supermarket and sit cross legged on the sawdust floor counseling their sullen children, "Do you *really* want to be sticking your fingers through the cellophane wrap on the ground chuck?"

Lawyers from New Jersey and their wives in unisex resort wear line the sidewalks rubbernecking network newsmen who jog into town for the *Times*. Ex-cabinet members and Presidential advisers have cocktails on the redwood decks of the colleagues they've left behind at Harvard and no one cares more for dressing than to throw a sports coat over what they've worn to pick blackberries. You'll see an occasional Mercedes on Main Street. On a cloudy day a Cadillac full of time-sharing condo owners from Harwichport might pull through on their way to Provincetown to show their houseguests the gays. But the rule is a Ford station wagon, stored on blocks over the winter at a pond-front plot bought in 1954 at twelve hundred dollars – with the house – that is now worth one-and-quarter million.

Wellfleet.

On any given summer morning Main Street turns into a drive-in movie parking lot, a frozen field of packed cars facing the post office from six directions. The lot has spaces for ten, and in winter, observing local tradition, people get their mail, peruse it quickly, say howdy to their neighbors, and leave. In summer, entire families park, run through the post office front door and disappear through the back to go shopping. German tourists unload their bikes and coast to the beach. Retirees back in their Winnebago vans. The spry second wives of New York analysts, their children leaning on the horns of vehicles double parked in the middle of the street, cuss out grizzly local oystermen bottlenecked behind them proving that nothing hones rudeness and guile like shopping at Zabar's.

But all of the time whatever you place in the work must do double or triple labor; it must have a reason for being there. Descriptions may fill us in on attitudes of the characters, their background, their relationships, according to what is chosen to put in and what is left out. Here the description of an upcoming birthday gives us the class and ethnic background of the characters, the closeness of the relationship between mother and daughter, the distant relationship between father and the same daughter.

From *Storm Tide*:

Yirina had baked both cakes and decorated them. She had sent Judith into Prospect Park where the daffodils were in bloom, to cut some and hide them in a bag pinned into her old coat that no longer properly buttoned. They looked lovely in the vases Yirina had brought with her from Mexico. Yirina had taken out the good tablecloth she always washed by hand, with fine embroidery of birds and flowers. Yirina had had it since her years in Turkey, during The War. Judith's mother could always make a feast. She could make a celebration out of a chicken, a couple of candles and a bottle of cheap Chianti. She could make a celebration out of a sunny afternoon and tuna fish sandwiches in Prospect Park. For Judith's father, Dr. Silver, she was wearing her best red dress of real silk and the diamond necklace that went in and out of the pawnshop several times a year. It was very important that they please Dr. Silver. Judith wondered if she ever really pleased him. Was he happy she existed? Did he wish she had never been born? She was always covertly staring at his square face, impeccably shaven, and trying to read his feelings for her.

Once again Judith unwrapped the flowered skirt that her mother had wrapped in the same paper, carefully opened the night before. Dr. Silver was a stout man of medium height, a bit stooped. His hair was all white, even the hair that bristled from his nose and ears. His eyes were a pale luminous blue, but Judith had dark eyes like her mother. Sometimes she tried to find herself in her father. She had her mother's dark hair, her mother's pale skin with an olive tint. Dr. Silver was ruddy. She was small like her mother, small for her age. Her mother could pretend she was ten for several years longer, when they occasionally went to the movies. But she had her father's hands, what Yirina proudly called "a surgeon's hands." Long-fingered but quite strong. She had his long narrow feet. Her mother's feet were small but wide. Her mother wore size 5C, a size they looked for in sale bins or rummage sales at the nearby churches of Brooklyn.

My apprentice writing was full of scenes described only because I found describing them interesting, and I suspect that is surely true of a number of you. You may write such descriptions as an exercise, but do not include them in your finished work unless they really belong there.

Similarly, if you are writing a memoir, the specifics you include will tell us a great deal about your family and your friends. They are precious to you because they are part of what formed you, but only your language and your choice of detail can make them precious to us. It is a case of persuading us that we care whether the kitchen of your childhood home had tan and gold squares of linoleum or terracotta tile on the floor; whether your bedroom curtains were filmy white or blue velvet; whether you slept with a teddy bear or a Barbie doll or a live tabby cat. You must make us care. You have to involve us in your life and involve us in the meaning, the resonance of these memories through vivid sensory language that carries an emotional message, and through an ongoing story that carries us forward.

Avoid words like *beautiful, pretty, ugly, handsome,* unless you do the work to make the scene or the painting or the man or the horse beautiful or ugly or whatever. Learn to describe briefly or in snatches, so as not to stop the story in an obvious way.

Make your descriptions work overtime to give us local color, reveal character, move the plot along, set us in time and place, fill in the socioeconomic picture, hint at the habits of the characters as they react to their surroundings.

From *City of Darkness, City of Light*:

Here is Georges Danton arriving in eighteenth-century Paris for the first time, without money but with great ambition and greater energy:

> The coach dumped him on the edge of Paris, in a slum festering under a black cloud of pestilent smoke. As he hiked through the narrow streets carrying his two portmanteaux, he choked from the stench of shit and rotten garbage. He was suffocated and deafened at once. In the perpetual twilight of the open sewers between dark houses sealing out the sky, every half block some poor soul was singing at the top of his lungs, bawdy songs, ballads of adventure and crime, topical songs, religious songs: all seeking sous from passersby and selling song sheets, scraping away on violins or banging on drums. Women carrying racks of old clothes pushed through the crowds. Swarms of beggars, crippled, blind, maimed, clutched at him. A man slammed into him. He watched his purse. Two men glared; he glared back. He elbowed his way along. Toughs looking into his scarred face saw someone who would readily fight. They let him pass.

I remember the opening of a memoir written in one of our workshops where the Greek old world character of the family was given to us through a description of smells of cooking and the food served at a meal characterized by high tension and drama. The emphasis was on the drama, but the food gave us necessary background that made the conflict more understandable.

Sometimes description does even more than that, because the land-scape is an actor in the drama. The landscape itself may be a presence as vivid and as important as any other character. In Stanislau Lem's *Solaris*, the ocean on the planet is alive and active in the novel. In Isaak Dinesen's autobiography, *Out of Africa*, Kenya is a vital part of the story of her marriage.

Sometimes "the city" or "the scene" is at the center of a novel, whether it is Hollywood or New York or Paris or Alexandria; and the city must be made new and bright and vivid in those stories. The city may be the destroyer or the seducer or the prize. But it cannot be merely alluded to; it must be recreated. This is equally true in fiction and in memoir. You must make Cleveland or Seattle vivid to us. The story of the writer who goes to Hollywood and is destroyed or falls into temptation and then recovers his or her integrity is an American cliché, but like all such stories, able to be told and retold, so long as it is made new and the seduction of the place is created for us so we experience it with the protagonist. We returned a recent submission from a retired professor of English whose description of Chicago was as flat as the city itself. We explained that many major cities have horrific traffic and large parks and rivers running through them and that her Chicago, a place of immense local character, could have been any one of them. She wrote back that we must have mistaken her book for another submission; that in Chapter One she specifically mentioned Grant Park and the Wrigley Building. Sorry, not enough.

Descriptions of people may function to tip us off to the attitude of the character doing the looking, the describing. It may contain enough attitude to suggest something of what is going to happen:

From *Three Women*:

The next year there was a new student who transferred in from Kansas. They both had history with him. He wasn't a jock, a club kid, one of the super students who ran the school, or a burnout who would be tossed, but like them, one of the weird kids. He was between them in height and had pale sleek blond hair he wore to his shoulders. His eyes were a dark haunting blue. He had a scar through one light brown eyebrow. His cheekbones were high and sharp, and his profile looked to her as if it should be carved on the prow of a sailing vessel. He always had shadows of stubble on his cheeks that made him seem older, more experienced. Half the guys had just started shaving. Evan had a darkish beard but not much of it. He only had to shave every other day, and it took him about a minute, although she did like to watch, cause it was such a male thing to do. She was almost hairless on her body and never even shaved her legs. To each other, they called the new kid the Decadent Viking. "I want him," Evan said.

"So do I," she said. "We'll share him."

They made up stories of capturing him, tying him up and doing things to him. His name was Chad. It seemed a silly name for such a fascinating-looking guy. He was broody. He sat at the back, and even when he knew the answers, he sounded as if he resented being right. She sat down next to him in assembly one day. His wrists stuck out below his shirt. There was a scar on each of them. He caught her looking at his wrists. They stared at each other. He did not hide his wrists. Then he smiled.

If you grew up in Toledo, Ohio, you have to work hard to make it interesting to us; but not if you grew up in Toledo, Spain. Then we want many sensory details of your growing up. If you introduce an exotic locale in your memoirs, we expect that locale to play a part in the story. We expect somehow that the story of growing up as the son of a missionary in the jungle of Paraguay will be different from the story of growing up as a minister's son in Dubuque, Iowa. If it is not different, that too is important to the narrative. If your family recreated a little Dubuque in the jungle, that's part of your story, and you want to make that real to us with vivid and emotionally engaging description.

Here is the beginning of a novel about a fourteen-year-old girl who spends all her free time in cyberspace. We are quickly and efficiently placed in the Philippines and given her family situation.

From *leo@fergusrules.com* by Arne Tangherlini:

I insist on durian. I love the sweet taste of the meat, and the rotten cheese stench of the skin keeps the curious from my room. I have the maid bring it up twice a day and leave it outside my door. When you're chasing Genghis Khan across the Tekla Makhan or gouging the eye from a Cyclops, the last thing you need is to be called down for supper – especially when it's a plate of hard rice and chicken overcooked in vinegar and soy sauce.

I wrote that in my journal ten months ago when I arrived in Manila. At the time, I was battling my grandmother, Lola Flor, who wanted to impose her medieval notions of order on me. In her house, every day was regulated according to the canonical hours of a monastery: breakfast was served at lauds, just as the sun rose; I left for school at prime; we recited the rosary right after I came home from school at none; we sat down to supper at vespers; and at complin Lola marched around the house turning out the lights. At school, she wanted me to listen for the bells of St. Andrew's and take my lunch when terce sounded, but that meant eating during math class. I tried it once just to see what would happen. I'd no sooner unwrapped my chicken wings than Mrs. Siew sent me to the principal's office.

In descriptions, it is the language that tips us off as to what is happening, the connotations of the words that tell us what to expect, subliminally, the way a score in music will set a mood in a film of suspense, impending doom, romance, serenity. The connotative language is the movie score working on you as you read. The shorter the description, the more power you must build into each word, the harder each phrase must work. Chapter One of *Lycanthia* by Tanith Lee begins with the description of a fast-moving train passing through a pastoral scene of villages and farms, then suddenly plunges into a land of winter, of ice and emptiness and sinister black forests. As the protagonist steps from the train at his station stop, the air is so sharp and cold, he can hardly breathe and the train's whistle seems to cry as it leaves him absolutely alone. Such a description connotes imminent harm; a land where nothing familiar, and probably nothing good, will happen.

Exercise

Write a one paragraph description which is powerfully connotative, which is leading to a murder, a frightful revelation, a disaster. Do not tell the reader what you are trying to convey but do it by language and the objects you choose to describe.

Exercise

Write a one paragraph description in which you convey the emotional attributes of a place; the way it makes you feel or the way you remember it, the way you want the reader to feel about it: fearful, angry, cozy, lost. It can be a room, a neighborhood, a school, a town, a large city. Don't name the emotion but attempt to choose words and images, objects and sensual details that may trigger the reader's own feelings about the place.

Exercise

Write a short scene in which your viewpoint character is encountering a different person. Give us a strong sense of a that person through what you choose to include about them – perhaps their clothing, their walk, the way they hold your stare or avoid your eyes. What do they smell like? What are they clutching? How do they act in the presence of other people: a bag lady? a cop? Here you are using description to characterize.

9

When You Have
Research to Do

FREQUENTLY YOU MAY have a fair amount of research to do on a novel or a personal memoir. Although there are a few sources particularly useful for personal narrative, there is a great deal of overlap and similar technique no matter what you are writing. For *Woman on the Edge of Time*, I had a lot of studying to do about the brain and psychosurgery, about how it feels to be in a mental institution, and a lot of research preliminary to thinking about the technology in a good future society. For *The Longings of Women* I needed to study homelessness and murder trial procedure in Massachusetts; I had to make on-site visits to several neighborhoods that are featured in the novel, the Barnstable House of Corrections, the courtroom where Becky's trial takes place, Lesley College where Leila teaches.

But some novels take an enormous amount of research. While I was writing *The Longings of Women*, I was already doing research on the French Revolution for *City of Darkness, City of Light*. It has a huge computer database, as did *Gone to Soldiers*, my World War II novel. The database for *Gone to Soldiers* was seven times as long as the novel itself. The database for the French Revolution novel covered thirty-two high density discs.

Searching a database on a computer is fast, but it still takes time.

115

However, it sure beats writing things in a notebook, where you have to go through everything to find anything. It beats ordinary file cards, because when each piece of information in a filing system depends on spatial location, either in a file drawer or in a card box, you can only get at that particular goody by one path, one label. It is under WOMEN or it is under HISTORY or it is under NINETEENTH CENTURY or it is under FRENCH COMMUNE or it is under LOUISE MICHEL. Some of those descriptors will prove useful at different times, but you might want a system that will get you that little goody by any of those routes.

Whatever system you end up using, I recommend some system to you. It is simply not useful to have the stuff you want and need on random pieces of paper, the backs of grocery lists or lost in the middle of a notebook. The disadvantage of that method, or lack of it, is that you wade through pages of extraneous stuff – stuff that was interesting enough to you when you wrote it down to make it likely you'll get suckered into reading it again now. There goes the afternoon.

I clip periodicals heavily and keep files on subjects possibly useful. Novelists are hungry for information. I am always way behind clipping things, let alone reading them. My house is always full of glaciers of yellowing newsprint creeping through the rooms. Perhaps half the subjects I clip will never become novels, but some of them will, and what I save (I tell my very skeptical husband whenever we move stacks of old magazines to pinpoint the odor of a long-petrified mouse) will eventually be useful for me.

Most of my fiction is research intensive and even my memoir required a great deal of digging. But as we've mentioned many times, all writers approach the subject differently. Some are absolutely fascinated by their own lives and do no research at all. Some work directly from memory, some from snippets of inspiration. In the preface to *The Spoils of Poynton* Henry James talks about the problem of hearing too much about an incident, what he calls the "futility of fact." He was at a lavish Christmas dinner one night in London when another guest mentioned in passing that an acquaintance of hers was "at daggers drawn" with her only son over the ownership of the furniture in an old house the son had inherited upon his father's death. James was immediately stung with an idea for a story, "as if the novelist's imagination winces at the prick of some sharp point." As the guest went on with specifics, however, his imagination began to fizzle. James compared that initial story idea to a newborn baby, with all the potential that metaphor implies, but as she proceeded to supply him with helpful details all she managed to do was "strangle it in the cradle even while she pretends, all so cheeringly, to rock it." Other writers mine their jobs for story ideas. Ira became a waiter, designed computer games and ran for public office in preparation for his three novels. The great critic Edmund Wilson used to research long articles about a subject before he tackled a book, a common practice today for non-fiction writers for the *New Yorker*, for example.

Interviewing is an undervalued art. As someone who has a lot of experience with being interviewed, I can tell you it is something usually done poorly. It requires empathy and direction, tact and a sense of tactics, patience and flattery. The best interviewer I have ever experienced is Studs Terkel; the best I've ever watched in action is Barbara Walters on TV. Both are extremely skilled and both massage and stroke the object/ victim/ target. Neither means harm but both are relentless and yet open, curious, for the moment a little in love. Love is a form of attention and so is interviewing.

I often ask people who have a specific expertise in an area I have written about to look over an entire novel or sections of the novel, to see if I have committed obvious gaffes, if I have handled the language or the jargon essential to one or more characters idiomatically. As we mentioned in the chapter on dialogue, you want to master some of the jargon of a profession, but only use it as flavoring. You do not want to create something so dense that your reader has to take a course to read what you have written.

I asked a historian who had been a bombardier during World War II (and before that had worked in a shipyard) and his wife, who had been a Rosie the Riveter, to go over *Gone to Soldiers* before the final draft and give me feedback on anachronisms. I also had a friend who was in New York during the war check out my milieu details. I had both a Holocaust survivor and a Holocaust scholar check relevant chapters. One of my old French professors checked my French and saved me some real gaffes. I had two other friends who had experienced different aspects of the war check the manuscript also. In spite of that, a couple of errors got through; some of them I have heard about from readers and was able to correct in the paperback – about five boners, as I recall. A copy editor should have caught at least the most important of those, but they usually spend their time fighting with you about points of grammar they imagine they know more about than you do – and missing grievous errors you would be pitifully grateful if they caught. Copy editors are mad for commas but not so interested in fact checking.

Most of your research you'll have to do at the library, through interlibrary loans, through on-site inspections and visits. You can get bibliography and some sorts of research off the internet, but books are the most convenient and efficient way to find out what you want to know. The internet is great for medical information, I've found, but not so great on history. However, there are listserves for almost every conceivable subject, and you can put queries on ones you join.

If you need to interview people, do them the courtesy of finding out as much as you can about them before you meet. Do not lie and do not get caught in oily flattery, but act even more interested than you are. You are taking up someone's time and you owe it to them to be prepared on your subject. Never try to make a person replace reference work. It is not right to ask someone to answer questions you could do yourself with an hour in the local library. Remember also that what people remember is highly selective and highly subjective.

Understand that we create the past and recreate it as we examine it. Even small facts are often unknowable. Again, using *Gone to Soldiers* as an example, there is a convoy in the third Duvey chapter, "The Black Pit." I researched the list of ships in that convoy in Washington and in London and in every available historical record; every single list was different. This is a well attested to convoy that should be a piece of cake to track. History fades under our hands. History changes. You must get used to entering the realm of the Maybe So. The finally unknowable.

Although this seems almost too obvious to mention, one of the worst things you can do is borrow a piece of equipment and use it for the first time while conducting an interview. I can't tell you how many interviews have failed because the interviewer was unfamiliar with the tape recorder or microphone and wasted at least fifteen minutes of the hour available fiddling with the equipment. If you must borrow equipment, use it first at home and try it out until you are familiar with it. Be sure you have enough cassettes with you. Be sure you are carrying spare batteries. You would be surprised how many interviews are lost because of mechanical failure on the part of the interviewer. You want your recorder to be unobtrusive, just sitting there quietly recording. You don't want to be monkeying with it, calling attention to it, stopping a natural flow to make sure you are recording properly. Be alert for the time you must turn the tape or change the cassette. You cannot reasonably expect any person to repeat what they have already said. If they told a great story full of charming detail the first time, they will give you a dry synopsis the second.

In writing a memoir, you may imagine you do not need to do research, but memory is fallible and you want the flavor of the times as well as the facts. To jog your own memory or even that of someone you know, try songs from the period in question. Often songs are associated with an era of our lives. Movies work less well, but they may work for you. Smells – the smell of a particular flower or perfume or soup – can jumpstart your memory. That usually happens without conscious preparation, but you can use a scent to recapture a period.

Old magazines (often available in libraries and sometimes on microfilm) can prove extremely useful in recalling or creating details; so can newspapers. By looking at ads or illustrations, you might recall your mother's dress or your father's hat, or some particular outfit you were dressed in. Ads are useful. So are news stories of the time. Such research can provide you with vivid details, the bits of image, of sound and phrase that make the past real to your readers – because they make it real to you.

Doing research with your family when you are writing a memoir or a piece about your family requires persistence and tact. You need to keep focused on what you are trying to find out (unless you are simply interested in recording everything). Mostly you won't have trouble getting people in your family to talk, once you have persuaded them that you are genuinely interested; but there are stories they do not want to tell, and often those are the ones you want to hear. It takes persistence and it takes tact and it takes a kind of flattering attention, but you will probably succeed in the end. Transcribing interviews, by the way, is one of the most tedious and annoying activities you will engage in and by far the least fun element of your research. But unless and until you transcribe interviews and notes, they are useless to you. I have known people who did many interviews but never wrote a book or even an essay, because they could not bring themselves to deal with the cassettes they had accumulated.

Sometimes reading a children's book that was important to you may bring back pieces of your childhood. Was there a radio program you listened to regularly or a television program you always watched? Did your family regularly watch some program together? Sometimes you can even find videos for sale of old TV programs that have some significance to you and may be useful. I found cassettes of news programs from World War II that were invaluable.

If you cook a particular dish that your mother or grandmother made, that too may bring back memories you have forgotten or render sharper and with far more significant sensual details some memory you do possess. Old photographs are an obvious source of information and emotion. You may use them to refresh your memories and use them as a device to get someone else in your family to talk about a particular family member or a particular era or event in which you are interested. You never know what may help. I have a tin box of buttons I took from my mother's sewing drawer after she died. I have found that certain of those buttons inadvertently brought back entire experiences because they recalled to me what my mother had worn on some special day or trip we had taken and which gave me an entire scene. I have a poem called "Unbuttoning" that came from that tin of buttons. For you, perhaps sports memorabilia, old comic books, a book of period toys, rock or movie posters might help. If you jitterbugged or waltzed, doing it to the right music could bring to mind bygone times and faces.

Experiment and see what may work for you. These are all only suggestions, but try out whatever you think might do the job.

10

A Scandal in the Family

E VERY BOOK HAS A STORY behind it that is usually as interesting as the book itself. Whether it's the adventures of the author's research trips or the fights with her editor; the grant money that was cut at the last minute or the shipment of galleys we received from the printer – missing all punctuation – I never tire of trading these stories at sales conferences and writers' workshops.

Because with every success recounted – and a published book, no matter how disappointing its sales may be, is a success – I take away hope for publishing another. The story of *The Kitchen Man* has been interesting to writers in our workshops who have faced issues of writing about people they love or in some cases failing to write because they could not face these issues. In most workshops, I'm asked to read the offending material, so it is included in the appendix of this book.

In the winter of the year I turned thirty years old, I was drinking a great deal of bourbon and listening to Bessie Smith albums every night upon returning from a job building a house. For one hour every morning, long before first light, I would climb out of bed, make a pot of strong coffee, feed the cat Jim Beam, whom I'd named after the bourbon, and work on a novel about a waiter. It was called *The Kitchen Man*, named after the Bessie Smith song. I had been a good waiter (I judge this by my tips, which were sizable) but a complete failure at the building trades (I judge this by the number of times I was ordered to remake windows I had framed, and once, a sleeping loft, which seemed to sway in mid-air like the gang plank in a Popeye cartoon). My mind was occupied. I was thinking about the novel all the time, stopping to scribble jokes on scraps of wallboard, muttering conversations I would, the following morning, assign to my characters. In this way I managed to complete and revise a four-hundred-twenty-five-page draft in a little over a year. It was good enough to get me a prestigious New York agent, which I defined at the time as someone who had at least one client who had written a best-seller and took me to lunch in a restaurant with a wine list.

For the next two years, the book made its way to twenty-four mainstream publishers. Their rejections ranged from the condescending ("Mr. Wood is a writer whose next book just might be good") to the absurd ("I cannot publish this book because I hate the protagonist. He reminds me too much of myself."). I was aware at the same time of a disjointedness of opinion that I could not dismiss. Many people who read the novel – I am talking here about other writers, some quite famous ones, and avid readers, as well as audiences who heard excerpts at readings – liked it very, very much. I kept being told how the book spoke to them of families like their own, of body types and neuroses like their own, of what they always feared went on inside pretentious restaurant kitchens, of people they recognized from life but not literature.

But my failure to place the novel had its advantages. For although I was a moody, envious, border-line alcoholic, given to pitiful, stentorian sighs (literary biographers will note that my wife's output, prolific by any standard, increased greatly when I got an office outside the house) the fact that I was not published saved me from a confrontation with my mother and father who were realistically, if not sympathetically, rendered characters in the book. It was certainly the case that the guilt I felt about what I had written had made me ambivalent about seeing it in print. When the agent gave up on the book, I refused to follow my wife's advice to submit it to an independent press that might have been open to something quirky and not recognizably commercial. I told myself it was either a big time New York City publisher or nothing.

After a year and another draft in which I cut a hundred pages, I did send it out to two small presses. Within a month I received an acceptance letter from the Crossing Press, then in Trumansburg, New York, and a few weeks later a contract. I was real. I was to be a published novelist, and if it was with a publisher many people outside the business had never heard of, this fact might work in my favor. My parents, who encountered books mostly in airports and suburban malls, were never likely to come across it. When my mother and I spoke, I never denied that it was going to be published, I just never mentioned it. I was working as an artist in the schools at this time and as a sixth grade teacher phrased the question in the fetid confines of the faculty lounge as I announced its publication to my colleagues, "Who the hell cares about a book published in a place called Trumansburg?"

At least one person did. The publicist. He had two essential qualities that elevated him, in my mind, to the best publicist I have ever worked with: he loved the book and he was fearless on the phone. At that time there was no Oprah's Book Club but if there was he would have tracked her to the ends of the earth. He sent it everywhere – the *New York Times,* the *Washington Post,* the *Toronto Globe & Mail* – followed up doggedly, and it worked. The wacky small press novel about an overweight gourmet waiter was widely reviewed. Not long after pub date, I got a call from my mother. "Why didn't you tell me your book came out?"

"You mean the *Kitchen Man*?" Duh. "I don't know, Ma. I must've forgot."

"There's a big review in the Sunday *New York Times*."

But my parents only read the *New York Post*. I thought I was covered. "How did you know?"

"Your aunt called from Arizona. I'm going out now to buy the book."

"Don't do that!" I said. "What I mean is, a mother should never have to pay for her son's book. I'll send it to you." I had bought myself some time.

Up to that point, I had never had a conversation with my parents about the pain I had felt growing up; about their treatment of each other and their verbally poisonous fights. Whereas, looking back on my life now, coming of age as a suburban fat kid whose struggling parents were ashamed of him seems a humorous footnote, but at thirty years old the attendant anger was still so much a part of me that in writing my first autobiographical novel, I had to include it. There was no way to write about myself otherwise.

It took me a week to decide to send the novel off and during that time, I came up with the scheme of using a razor blade to neatly delete

Chapter Four. But the publicity man was doing his job, capitalizing on good reviews to get even more print media attention. The book was gaining momentum. Paperback reprint offers from the large New York publishers were coming in. Movie producers were calling; so were the relatives. Before I got around to sending the book, my mother called to inform me that she had bought it. That she was liking it.

"Really! How far did you get?"

"Just up to Chapter Three."

I did not hear from her for some weeks after that. When I did finally force myself to call on Sunday morning, her response was predictably cool. "Oh, I got really busy. I stopped reading it," she said.

"How far did you get?"

"Chapter Four."

"Is that him?" I heard my father's rumbling behind her. He took the phone.

"Hi, Pop."

"Hey, I read your book."

"What did you think?"

"Well, you didn't treat me too bad."

"I didn't?"

"But you really socked it to your mother!"

The conversation ended. The momentum of the book continued. A movie option was negotiated. I agreed to be represented by the William Morris Agency. I signed a deal to write the screenplay for Universal Pictures. I still was not speaking to my mother about the book. It hurt me that my success had caused her embarrassment. But it troubled me, too, to feel that my experience was not mine to write about. Was it not my side of those years together? Didn't the right to tell the story of my own life belong to me?

My mother and I continued to have shallow, careful conversations until in one of them, many months later, she said, "Did you really feel that way about us? That we were so bad to you?"

I did. And yet I didn't. That is, they were my parents: I loved them and recognized that we had gone through some tough times together. I understood that my mother had married in her teens, and that my dad was just twenty years-old; that they themselves had difficult parents, that finances never ceased to be an issue. I understood all the reasons why they were the way they were. Because she had brought up the question, I was able to tell my mother that yes, it had been bad for me, but that I honestly felt they had always tried to do their best. I believe she heard that. I cannot say that we patched up all differences and became a tight mother and son. I can say that it was a start. From that point forward we stopped lying about the past; we acknowledged there had been some good times but by and large those years had been difficult for all of us.

My father read and reread the book and bought copies to give to friends. He was not a man who had a vocabulary to express such things, but I believe that seeing himself in print made him feel his days on earth had been documented and were therefore more important, that I had rendered his life as art. My brothers were amused by what I had written but not particularly moved. Years younger, they did not have the same experiences or, because my folks had managed to solve many of their problems and change over the years, the same parents. My writing was in no way prescient. Neil Simon, Phillip Roth and hundreds of other writers had been lampooning the Jewish-American experience for years. Still, my mother became very proud of her son the novelist and began to send me articles by children who had written about their families, often with a note that said, "Oh, what you wrote about me is nothing compared to this one." She even redefined our cheap relatives as those who took my book out of the library but wouldn't buy it. I have had the feeling moreover that my mother has been somewhat disappointed in my subsequent books because she was not in them.

I'm not about to revise the experience and pretend it was pleasant, but neither can I say I'm sorry. I wrote what I had to write. It was the truth of my side of the experience. It may have hurt my parents to read it, it may have embarrassed them, but it did not kill them. It did not cause them to suffer nervous illness. It did not make them lose their jobs. It did not cost them any friends. Growing up together was not easy for any of us. The novel bore witness to those difficult years. In the way shared tragedy sometimes does, it brought us closer together.

Writing about my family with emotional honesty and seeing it through to being published was my choice. Since every family is unique, I would never advise someone else to take this risk. In all our classes, and in the relevant essays in this book, we emphasize the various distancing techniques that writers sometimes use to write about those close to them. But simply changing a person's name or disguising their appearance and details about them is not always sufficient protection from charges of libel. You cannot make false or defamatory statements about living people. You cannot subject a person to undeserved publicity without permission. But the law is complex and we readily admit our ignorance. In all our workshops we warn participants about the possible legal implications involved in writing about real people. We mention the advisability of seeking out attorneys who specialize in intellectual property issues, libel and/or invasion of privacy. We offer the titles of books that can inform you about these issues and we strongly advise people to consult them.

But having mentioned the risks, there are certain things I've discovered for myself:

1. We live in a society in which the most heinous and embarrassing human behaviors are merely fodder for sitcoms and daily talk shows. What you may agonize about revealing might make the average reader yawn.

2. Revealing the truth as you see it might explain a person's life in a way that makes their behavior far more explicable than covering it over.

3. Sometimes people really don't mind being written about because you are enabling them to see their lives in a new perspective. My father read and reread my novel many times; my mother still gives away copies as gifts. Some people thought my parents were treated very callously in the book. My parents ultimately felt that I had helped them to understand their own lives, and our most difficult years as a family, from a different perspective.

4. Your job as a writer is to make people real. Cartoon characters and walk-ons don't make a story breathe. You've got to allow the reader to see a well-rounded picture of your important characters and that includes the contradictions in their personalities, all the surprising dualities that make each of us interesting and unique.

5. Most important to me is that by telling your truth you help readers accept the truth about themselves. By admitting that your family might have had problems, you're helping others out of their shame and

isolation. You're helping them understand that their lives might not be perfect, but that neither is anyone else's. There's a great backlash today about our confessional society. I admit, daytime TV talk shows and all the dependency literature have us wondering if people shouldn't keep their sordid histories private. But to my mind, it was worse in the 1950s when the archetypes of the solid American middle-class family bore no resemblance to the problems and the tensions I walked into when I came home from school, making me feel my family was a shameful secret.

6. There are many ways to view any experience. How you experienced a particular incident may be very different from someone else who was there.

7. In your memoir or your novel, you are writing, not for now, not for the evening news, or the weekly magazine, but presumably for years and decades to come. You are attempting to distill experience into art. What is tender and emotional now may not be so in time. You are banking on the fact that it is the rendering of events that is important; that the identity of the actors is less important than the play itself. You are attempting to fill the facts with meaning.

One last footnote on the publication history of *The Kitchen Man*. One might have thought that twenty-four rejections would have made me skeptical about large conglomerate publishing companies being the proper home for a comic literary novel. But the year after it came out, I was flush with all the attention and thought that a writer of my stature would be best served by a large New York publisher. Although the Crossing Press would have gladly brought out a paperback edition, I pressed them to sell the rights to a major paperback house. Over the years, the book slowly gained a following. I was being invited to read at colleges. In fact the book was being taught at some. One day my new editor called to tell me that she was sorry (she actually was) but she had just received notice that the book had been recycled and was no longer in print. Yes, it had been selling; but not enough to justify keeping it in inventory.

It's a strange experience to see a book of yours go out of print, to have two or three years of your life pulped. It's listed in your resume.

Academics mention it when they introduce you, but it's a little like a story you tell that you can never prove, or a deceased friend that exists in your memory only. When we started Leapfrog Press, we brought it back into print as our first book – partly because there was a continuing demand and partly because we were just learning how to publish and decided our early mistakes should be on our own work, not somebody else's.

By the way, no one was more upset when the book went out of print than my mother, who by that time was buying five or six copies every holiday season, and now had to begin the tedious search for new gifts.

11

Work and Other Habits

I N TALKING ABOUT BARRIERS to creativity, we are also talking about daily life and daily habits and how we live our lives in general and in particular, and also how we can help each other overcome these barriers.

One way to begin breaking down the inner barriers to creativity is in small local groups, in collectives, in workshops, with other writers who come together to try to keep each other working, productive, sane, alive, and who try to help.

What's most important in a workshop, whether a formal one or one you put together from an ad in a copy shop, is being committed to helping each other do what that writer wants to do, not what you want to do or what you think that writer should want to do.

Let's say you're in a workshop with other fiction writers. You write tough laconic prose and you like things to be dry and clear and crackly. Someone in the group writes about their childhood sexual abuse. This is emotional stuff and it is written about in an emotional way. It's everything you would never do on paper. Your natural response may be boredom, sarcasm, embarrassment or the intellectual equivalent. But that helps nobody. What you have to do is to distance yourself from your distaste and figure out how the writer can do what she is trying to do and do it better. It isn't anything you would ever write or even care to read, but you aren't *everyone*. If the other writer can pull it off, some people will want to read it. Your obligation in any workshop is to offer comments in good faith about how the writer can do what she wants to do, not what you want to do.

Another example: you loathe violence and are strongly for gun control. You can't imagine why any sane person would want a gun in the house. Another person in the group writes a cop procedural that has a lot about firearms in it. You would never pick this book up, but here you are listening to descriptions of how to bring down a suspect without deadly force and with it. Nobody is asking you to join the NYPD. But you owe it to your fellow participant in the workshop to listen carefully or read carefully and give that writer the feedback that will enable him to write a better police procedural, not an anti-gun tract.

We can help each other in small and undramatic, daily, weekly, monthly ways. We can help by being ready to listen. We can help by reading each other's manuscripts. Often it is easy to get friends to read something in print – everyone wants a copy of a book, not understanding the author is limited to a small number of copies depending on contract – but very few are really willing to put the time into a manuscript. (They may insist that they are, but just wait and see how long it gathers dust beside their bed.) Yet that is the one important time for input. After a book is printed, criticism is interesting but not useful for improving the object. When a book is in manuscript, it can still be altered. Then is the time that criticism, that the willingness of others to read and to be generous with their time and involvement, is most meaningful.

We can help when another writer has trouble working. In Vermont several women I know formed a small group. They worked together in the same house, so that each kept the others working, prevented the giving way to temptations or interruptions. It was a fixed time for work and nothing else. In addition, they read each other what they had written at fixed intervals and gave each other vital feedback.

In Chicago, when I was completely unknown and quite invisible, I joined other unknown writers, African-American and white, in a small group that met regularly and gave each other criticism and hope. Without that small group, I don't think I would have stopped writing, but I would have written more slowly.

Parents can form a playgroup with other writers who have children.

This would free up certain days for work at the cost of perhaps one day a week. Where there is a willingness to help each other, a commitment to midwifing each other's creativity, we will find ways.

I feel guilty if I don't write, but I observe that sometimes writers who view writing primarily as self-expression may feel that writing itself is an indulgence. A person may even feel guilty about writing. Nobody asks you to do it to begin with – to create something new. You're solely responsible for the content, which may be revealing and contrary to how you're told you should feel. I wonder how many writers are afraid that what they want to say will hurt their family – will upset their partner, their mother or father; perhaps their children will be disturbed and offended.

But most importantly when you sit down to write, you imply that what you are saying, what you choose to take the time and space and paper to say, is more important than anything else you could be doing at the moment in service to others. Tillie Olsen has written eloquently about the long silence of women – about the heartbreaking times of trying to combine mothering, working, and writing and how she lost much of what she wanted desperately to create. Time, time, unbroken chunks of time.

We may be taught only certain emotions are permissible to express. When we begin to write, we may find those old inhibitions and prohibitions now internalized as a censor, changing the work in revision or else stopping it before it can get out. The inner censor sets limits to what I dare to say of what I feel and know and see and think. Self-censorship for all writers has similar roots. You are afraid on one hand that people will say, that's ridiculous. Nobody acts that way (except you.) No one else feels that way toward her child/spouse/lover/mother. You have to have a commitment to the truths wrung from yourself as well as the truths already made public by common struggle or history.

For women many of our experiences were dumb to us, unnamed, unpossessed because misnamed. I had insights at fifteen that I would seize again at twenty-six and lose because I had no intellectual framework in which they might fit and be retained. As writers we are always asking in public through our work whether our experiences and those of other people with whom we empathize and from whom we create, are experiences common to at least part of the population, or whether the experiences we are working with are singular, bizarre. There are inner censors that make shallow or imitative or tentative or coy the work of a writer, often through fear.

Voices speak in our heads that tell us we are brazen to admit certain things, that we should be ashamed. We may fear to offend those with power over us or hurt those whom we wish to love us or those whom we wish to please. We may fear what those whose politics or religion we share and whose good opinion we rely on may say about work which deals with a contradiction in our mutual politics or religious values, and the contradictions between ideology or belief and action. Yet such contradictions are rich to writers. Often we grasp our characters most firmly in those moist irrational interstices between intention and delivery, between rhetoric and greed, between image and fear.

Shame can get in creation's way. We all have notions of what we should be. A writer had better have considerable tolerance for that gap between what we would like to be and what we are in a daily way; at the same time, I think it helps a writer to have experience of how extraordinary people can be in situations that stretch them utterly. Sometimes we are ashamed of what moves us or how much we are moved; at other times we feel we ought to have been moved and we try to pretend. We don't only fake orgasms; people have faked orgiastic appreciation of many things that bored and even affronted them, from the Grand Canyon to their party's heroines and rhetoric, to the current literary fad or lion.

As a poet and as a novelist, I have to believe that when I go into myself honestly to use what I find there, that it is going to speak to you. Some of our experiences are similar and some are different, but the naming of both liberates us. The recreating of the experiences, the using of the feelings that may be different feels more dangerous to me, as if I may stand alone in that saying; yet I think these experiences are important too for us. So much of our lives have been lived in the dark, in ignorance of what others think and feel and experience. Many of our notions about what others' lives are like are simplified images from the media.

Exercise

Often we ask participants in a workshop to sit in silence and think about their lives and what they have written about, and then to think of something that made them ashamed or afraid, that they have never written about. Something they were reluctant to share with others. You might want to make a list of subjects about which you have never written – not lions and tigers and earthquakes and space travel, but things inside yourself, the hidden or secret side of yourself. After you have finished a short list, read it to yourself and imagine what or how you might write about one of those items on the list. Do you need to employ one of the distancing techniques we spoke of in an earlier chapter? Fictionalize it? Use third person? Create an alternate universe? Do you need to seek permission to tackle it from someone you love? From yourself? Do you feel you might need legal advice?

Suppose that a person writes what she must. That is only the first step in being a writer. The work must survive the moment of its creation. It must get out to an audience. She or he must dare to show the work. She must risk ridicule, misunderstanding, scandal, condemnation, and what's often worse, none of the above: silence. No attention at all.

Many people do manage to write, but then hide their writing. This is writing as self-expression, but not as communication. There can be no feedback, no sense of success or failure, no sense of outreach, of impact on the world. This is to act, but to pretend not to have acted and take no consequences for one's act.

Occasionally one reads of parents who have a baby and then shut up that child in a room. (I know you would only read these papers while standing in the checkout line of the supermarket, of course.) The tabloid headline reads. "Diapered 23-year-old Found in Cleveland Apartment, Chained to Playpen." I suppose it comes from not cutting the umbilical cord.

Once the work is done, it's ready for its own life. Your art is not you. It exists on its own. Others will take it, use it, abuse it, carry it off. It is their right to do so. There is a necessary letting go in artistic production, a point when you permit what you have made to depart from you and begin its own history. You will hear from it, or more accurately, hear about it from time to time in a fan letter, a hate letter, a review. However, it's not *you* but *it*. There must be some mental discipline to make this distinction, a very important one for preserving sanity.

Writers who meet together to support and criticize each other's work can easily spawn readings – anyplace, at bookstores, at coffeehouses, at schools, in nursing homes and hospices, in restaurants, at universities and libraries, in galleries, at festivals. Often groups or cooperatives of writers can get readings that would never be available to any particular unknown or little known writer. Some groups have also published their own anthologies or started magazines. The number of writers who first published themselves is larger than you might imagine, but it is far more effective to self-publish as a group and often achieves more visibility and better distribution.

You may get frustrated by the size of a small audience, but believe this: even the best selling and most respected writers are sent on tours and into malls where six people show up for a reading, half of whom wandered in by accident. It's part of the business and you can never predict whether the date you scheduled six months before turns out to be game seven of the World Series or, as one of our writers discovered the day he did the *Fresh Air* show and expected a large crowd at a popular suburban bookstore, the final episode of *Survivor*. However, in a group of five or six, each writer can generally bring (coerce) five or six friends to come and listen. That makes a sufficient audience for beginning readers to practice on.

If reading to an audience gives you stage fright, practice on each other. Shout, yell, let go, emote, sing your work. Borrow, share a tape recorder and listen to yourself. If you find yourself dull, an audience will wither. Learn to get inside the poem or the story. Think of the work not of yourself, and make it shape itself on the air. Make people hear it. Practice and practice some more. Readings are one of the best ways for you to reach an audience, and if you have published something, that's one of the best ways to get people to buy it. People will seldom pick up a book by an author whose name does not strike a familiar chord, but after a reading, if people in your audience have enjoyed it, often they want a book as a souvenir of the experience, as a way of revisiting what moved, amused or stimulated them.

You want to write, but you might be having trouble doing what you want to do; perhaps that's what drew you to this book. In a workshop, there is a point on the last day when I ask participants to think critically about their situation. How is your time organized? Could you get up early in the morning and write? Could you write late at night when everyone else is asleep? Could you find some block of time on the weekends?

Do you have a place where you can really write? Is there a door that shuts, or at least a partition setting that space off? Many people get hung up on their equipment. Is the computer functional and the screen easy to read? Do you need a more up-to-date word processing program? It's easy enough to say that many great writers have had no more equipment than a legal pad, but no publisher we know would accept a submission of three hundred hand-written pages.

Sometimes the problem is eliminating a time-consuming ritual, or even harder, a small pleasure. Do you need to stop subscribing to the morning newspaper or at least stop reading it with your sharpest mental energy every morning? Should you swear not to turn on the TV certain evenings or during the day on weekends or other days off? Should you disconnect the phone or turn down the volume on the answering machine? Can you give up jogging or going to the gym on certain days to have time to write? You cannot do everything, so you must prioritize, and if you really want to write, you have to make time for it. Perhaps you need to give up a social activity or a meeting or two. Perhaps you have to decide, okay I'm not going to take off that ten pounds, but I will get my book written instead. Which means more to you? That's what it comes down to. It is always a matter of priorities. Many people ask the question how much time it really takes to write a book and they're surprised to hear us say, quite honestly, that one solid hour of concentration every day may be enough. Think about it. A page a day, 365 days a year is certainly enough for a first draft. Sometimes the worst thing you can do is allot too much time – time for fussing over individual words, time for rewriting perfectly functional sentences, for dallying on the internet or in the dictionary, in the bathroom, in the kitchen. One hour with your best energy every day can force you to focus, to get your sentences down on paper because there is no more time. It may be the one most productive hour in your entire day, the one you think about and take notes for. One hour. Before everyone else wakes up; or after they go to bed; or while they're all out to lunch.

Ira always tells the story in workshops of the woman who came up to him after we had finished presenting and asked him how she could change her life so that she could find time to write. He said, "Why don't you get up earlier in the morning and write then?"

She said, "But I already get up at five forty-five."

"So write then."

"I meditate. Then I run for an hour."

"Okay, after that."

She said, "I have breakfast, shower, get dressed and go to work."

"How about on your commute?"

"I have to drive."

"How about on your lunch hour?"

"I eat at my desk and then I go the gym."

"How about when you get home from work?"

"I have therapy on Monday, my group on Tuesday. . . ."

You get the idea. Her life was blocked out and she was not willing to relinquish any of her activities.

"Then you're screwed," said Ira.

We've all learned long ago that nobody can "have it all." Nobody. It's a myth. Writing, like a good relationship, time with your kids, a model's body, a Ph.d., a vacation in Maui – you name what turns you on – takes sacrifice. What are you willing to give up for that one hour a day?

What we ask people to do in workshops is to think seriously about how you organize your time and your space and to come up with one change that would enable you to do more of the writing you want to do. Not a vast change, like *I am going to quit my day job*. Rather a small change that you have some hope of carrying out. You are going to write down this intent on a piece of paper and put it in the corner of a mirror you use every day. In a month, you take it down and replace it with another intent, that can carry you a little further.

One of the major advantages you can carry away from a writing workshop or a writing course is simply a stock of questions to ask yourself, both before you begin on a piece, and while you are in progress, when things go wrong. Am I beginning in the right place? Does my beginning seduce the reader into wanting to continue? Do I know enough about my main characters? What are their longings? Are they motivated and convincing? The more conscious you are of the possible variables, the more control you have over what you are doing. You can avoid wasting large amounts of time and more importantly, your writing energy on false starts that do not produce viable work, by learning to do enough preliminary figuring out. You can also learn what to ask when you realize your narrative is not succeeding.

It is equally important not to begin a long work prematurely as it is not to delay starting it for too long. If you start too soon, you will waste a lot of time and energy writing from the wrong viewpoint or in the wrong person (first when it should be third, for instance), writing stuff that belongs in the dossier but not on the page. You have to allow time before beginning a longer piece, but you do not want to delay your launch until you have talked about it too much and lost interest in what you are doing. We all know people who were going to write a book about some subject dear to them but never in fact get around to doing it. You can talk out a book or a piece and lose the necessary momentum. Discussing a work you have not written may be necessary if you are seeking funding or an advance, but it is dangerous to do too much of it. Many a writer has had to repay an advance because by the time they got to actually writing the book they had been shopping around, they lost interest in the whole project. You also run the serious risk of being discouraged by other people in the early stages, when you are most vulnerable to criticism or simply a lack of enthusiasm.

When you have finished – usually not the first draft but what you imagine to be the last, although it may well not be – you need to plan to protect yourself from postpartum depression. It is an extremely real and menacing state which I have witnessed not only in myself but in many others, apprentice writers, those being published for the first time and writers in mid-career. I try to have another project on hand at that point – for me usually a book of poetry I am putting together, or some essays I meant to work on. Perhaps reviews I have been promising I will get to. A short article. A short story. My only play was written at such a time. Whatever you select, it is important you have something in the wings.

I try out manuscripts between third and fourth drafts on my agent for her feedback on whether or not the novel is ready to try to sell and her estimate of possibilities. Up until this time, no one at all will have seen the book except Ira Wood. I may have sent an excerpt to a magazine or read a chapter to an audience somewhere but the novel has not been seen by anyone, certainly no one in publishing. This is also the time I seek criticism and feedback from friends, colleagues, other writers whose opinion I trust, experts in something I'm dealing with and also from people I regard as good general readers – people who read a lot and can critique what they have read.

I wait that long to share what I have written with my agent partly because I do not want anybody telling me I can't tackle a particular subject or that something isn't commercial or sexy or fashionable or whatever before the work is essentially in place. It may need some tightening, some tidying, some trimming or perhaps some expanding, but it stands.

You must learn, once something is completed, to hustle for your work. You would not hesitate to push a little for a child or a lot for a business. Your work is an "other," once it's completed, and it deserves the same attention. It may be an unfortunate reflection of our times, and it is certainly ironic, given an art that attracts people who do most of their work absolutely alone, but a writer today has to be something of an entrepreneur, ready to market one's work if not oneself. This certainly means submitting it, again and again. It may mean getting yourself readings, writing query letters, learning to deal with rejections and on occasion insults. It may mean writing reviews, for print or on-line media, to make connections, to make deposits in the favor bank and to get your name known by readers and by publications who will be more likely to review you. As foolish as it may feel to spend half an hour yakking with a talk show host on a local cable channel who may or may not have read your book, or a radio disk jockey who certainly has not, you never know who is listening, who may become curious now or five books from now. It's well to remember that close to 60,000 books are published every year. You have to separate yourself from the pack by reading and signing books in libraries, in schools, at conferences; in mall stores where you may be asked to sit behind a stack of books at a card table, of no more interest, probably less, than the parakeets in the pet shop window. Do it; then laugh about it with other writers. If you push your work collectively, you may feel less shame, less guilt, which is another reason to have a group.

A writer must have the support of some kind of community in writing about her experiences, or she will feel crazy. A person who believes she is crazy will not write or will write perhaps but in a code. She may destroy what she has written because it is, she believes, bad – bad in not measuring up to standards she has been taught usually based on the work of men who grew up in the nineteenth-century or bad in a moral sense – wicked. A strong woman is still widely seen as a bad woman. A woman who internalizes such judgments – as to some degree all women raised in sexist societies do – will punish herself for her strengths as well as her weaknesses.

Similarly a man who writes may feel he is less of a man because he deals with feelings, emotions, the epiphenomena of the interior and daily life. Or simply because he does not go off to a job every morning as other men in his family have done. He may feel the need to counter the image of himself as wimp by acting twice as macho or writing twice as offensively as anybody else. He may accept the judgment that he is less of a man, less of a person, and thus less deserving of respect. For this he may blame himself, his mother, women in general or some woman who personifies the sex to him. We have seen examples of writers who've done all of the above. We all have emotions and inner lives, whether we choose to put them in a particular work or not. It is wise for a writer to accept that we all have strengths and weaknesses, virtues and vices, failed intentions and shameful fantasies as well as simply silly ones. We are all bundles of variant selves we may never have a chance to live out in the external world – and often for good reason.

Now, a work must be able to be conceived of before it can get past the inner censor and be written. We are limited to what we can imagine. What we do is partly determined by desire, partly by what we think will be the consequences, and partly by what we imagine are the possibilities we can choose among. We need to read widely and critically to study the craft of other writers. We also read because when someone has written about a particular subject or in a particular vein, it may prick our imaginations into new possibilities – not an imitation but a new direction that the other writer has opened up or simply rendered imaginable.

Basically good writing is done because it has to be done, because the person doing it cannot be dissuaded, distracted, ignored or punished into silence. It always happens against the odds. But you don't start back on square one. If art demands a long apprenticeship, it also offers the rewards of mastery, that what was once inconceivably difficult becomes second nature, and that always, always there is something more difficult and demanding asking to be tried. Our imaginations, our abilities may fail, but never the possibilities before us.

12

Practical Information for You

ONCE YOU HAVE FINISHED a piece of work, whether it is a memoir, a novel, a short story or a poem, what do you do with it? You've written it, revised it, perhaps tried it out on your writing group or a friend or ten friends. Now you're ready to test your luck at getting it published in some form.

First, some information that's almost too obvious to include, but you'd be surprised to learn that perhaps fifteen per cent of writers who submit to our press and all the various magazines and journals we have edited over the years don't include a self-addressed stamped envelope, an SASE. It does not matter if you want your manuscript back or not. If you do, be sure you include an envelope with sufficient postage for the weight of the manuscript. Don't guess. If you don't want it returned, you still want to know if the work is accepted or rejected. Always include an SASE. Some editors simply discard such unaccompanied manuscripts unread. If the writer isn't savvy enough to include an SASE, they are unlikely to pass muster in their work. Considering that even the smallest presses receive twenty to thirty manuscripts a week, you should not find it difficult to figure out why the SASE is a prerequisite to being considered. No press or magazine can afford return postage on the manuscripts that come to it.

We also see a great many manuscripts that do not put the writer's last name and a running short title at the top of every page. Apparently these writers too do not understand the volume of submissions all editors receive. The stuff falls on the floor. The cat knocks it over or it gets moved aside to make room for lunch. A wind blows through an open window. An earthquake occurs. Use your imagination. We have also received manuscripts that were unnumbered. How they expected anyone to keep that manuscript intact and in order is anybody's guess. If you make it difficult to read your submission, then the editor will be in no hurry to read it and may not bother at all. After all, you are in a pile with sixty to a hundred others. If yours offers particular problems, it will often go unread or be given only grudging attention.

Do not put your manuscript in a fancy package, use blue paper or pink ribbons or draw pictures unless they are part of your text. It is a turn-off to see a gussied-up manuscript. The editor suspects the manuscript needed that ribbon or that lavender paper to stand out.

Be sure your print-out is clear and dark. Again, no editor who has been reading manuscripts for six hours is going to bother with one that is hard to read. Don't imagine you can make the manuscript look shorter by using a smaller font. Every editor knows that trick and resents it. If your editor's eyes are tired, again she will not give your manuscript the reading you would desire. As we have said in the chapter on beginnings, you can count on an editor reading perhaps two pages of a short piece and perhaps ten pages of a long piece. If you haven't grabbed the editor's attention by then, you will not have a second chance.

Unless the editor asks you to, do not call the publisher. Frankly, it marks you as an over-anxious author who will be difficult to do business with and something of a pest. The postal service may not be perfect but it usually works. If you want to know if your manuscript arrived, enclose a postcard addressed to yourself. If you have not heard from a publisher, it is more than likely because they have not read your submission yet and will not be able to until they have the time. Once they have read it, you can be sure they will get back to you. If they like the book, they're excited about the possibility of signing it. If they don't, there is no advantage to keeping it in the office. Publishers know how much of an author's time and self-esteem go into a book. But authors should also know what goes into publishing a book There is an irony involved in the schedule of publishing that may account for the fact that many publishing offices are in a state of constant catch-up. Books are signed and announced about a year ahead of publication. The manuscript goes back to the author for revisions and returns to the editor just as another book is being signed and announced, so that publishers are almost always in a state of doing the tasks they had agreed to do six months ago and which are approaching deadline – writing catalog copy, presenting to the sales reps, overseeing cover copy, cover design, internal design, printing, galleys, sending out galleys, marketing, writing advertising and publicity copy, trying to get the book reviewed, trying to get readings and book-signings and interviews for the author. It's a costly and time-consuming process for large, independent and very small presses. Once a book is accepted, it goes to the head of the line and grabs the available attention, as it should. The manuscripts waiting to be read have to wait some more.

Rather than calling, it's better to send an e-mail to a publisher after consulting their web site if you are still unsure of what kind of submissions they are interested in. Or write a letter requesting their submissions guidelines (which can also almost always be found on the web). Once a manuscript is accepted or you are dealing with the publisher about contracts, calling makes sense. But before you actually have a relationship with a publisher, random calls may single you out as someone they do not want to do business with.

The best writer is one who meets deadlines and then does readings, interviews and other publicity. A book doesn't sell itself. Readings add value to a book; they give the bookstore and the potential buyer an evening of free entertainment. They add a personal dimension. In anticipation of a reading, a bookstore may order thirty or more copies of your book, display and advertise it. Two writers can be equally good. One will give as good a reading to the three people who show up on a snowy night in January as to a hundred. That same writer will solicit readings for herself and not simply sit there waiting for lightning to strike. That writer will sell books. The one who sits home will not.

Some publishers and magazines state that multiple submissions are fine with them; others state quite clearly that they are not. With these, you have to follow your own conscience. I know we used to permit multiple submissions, because as writers as well as editors we were sympathetic with how long it takes to get word back on a manuscript. Then we got stung. We read a novel, spent the time to critique it – and we are talking now about an investment of days, not hours – only to find that the writer had submitted elsewhere and was negotiating with someone else or had already sold the book, without telling us. No, we're not going to have the writer arrested for stealing our time; but neither are we likely to forget his name.

Always keep a record of where you send your work. Years ago I sent a submission to the *Minnesota Review.* The rejection slip came back with my poems, and the notation on it, *We did not care for these poems the first time we saw them and our opinion has not changed with time.* I was embarrassed and I had wasted my time and postage. Always keep a chart on the wall or a record on your computer of where your work has gone. If an editor rejects your work but sends an encouraging letter, do not send more work immediately. Wait a month or so and then send more, reminding them gently that they had encouraged your submission. Do not wait a year. The editor will have long forgotten your work; in fact, there may even be a new editor reading manuscripts.

Try to learn the name of the editor – perhaps by using one of the resources we recommend next. Address the note that accompanies your work to the right editor. Don't send fiction to the poetry editor or vice versa. If you have been published or won any awards, mention them. However, do not include workshops you have taken. Everybody in the business knows you can take a workshop with almost anyone, and it means nothing. Furthermore, you may be saying you took a workshop with George Fadoodle, and the editor hates him and has ever since Fadoodle wrote a bad review on his work. So you have put a strike against you when you needn't have. If you are submitting poetry, do not bother to say you had an article in the *New England Journal of Medicine*, no matter how prestigious that is in the world of doctors. Do not mention your articles in *Golf Digest.* Only literary work matters when you are submitting literary work. You can mention work in another literary genre than the one you are submitting this time, but that's all that counts.

For book-length fiction and memoir, in our experience, over-long cover letters, like packages that have enough tape on them to withstand a category three hurricane, mark the writer as an amateur. The function of a cover letter is to introduce yourself and your credentials and to provide a brief overview of the work. The work will stand up for itself. Nothing you say in the cover letter will convince the press to publish the manuscript. It will get read, if only the first few pages. There really is no reason to give a long detailed synopsis of the manuscript. The flap of a hardcover book is designed to arouse enough of your curiosity to make a purchase. Flap copy is approximately two hundred fifty words long, and is usually a good example of a well-written synopsis, but far too long for the synopsis of a cover letter. Have confidence, they will read it eventually no matter what your cover letter says. But a short, three-sentence synopsis is far better than a three-page single spaced outline of every chapter.

I don't know why, but cover letters seem to adhere to fashion; which led me to believe that some text book was telling writers to include marketing plans with their manuscripts. For about a year, they arrived in waves. While an author's marketing plan is certainly welcome once the decision is made to publish the book, especially if the author is serious in their promise to help the publisher carry it out – many authors, already on to their next book by pub date, do not want to be bothered – it seems somewhat pretentious when accompanying a submission. In any event, it is usually discarded.

There are certain things you can include that might give you a leg up. Most important is your publishing experience. Editors like to know your track record. If you have published before, include the books, magazines, publishers and dates. Some people without extensive publishing credentials include their education, but this is dicey. Whereas telling an editor you graduated from a famous writing program may offer some hope that the project which is about to consume her Saturday morning does follow some generally accepted conventions – deeply drawn characters, for instance – she may not, unless she has an affiliation with that program, care, and moreover, may not consider your college something to brag about. Many people who have succeeded in other professions include a detailed listing of their accomplishments – medical doctors are often guilty of this – but it doesn't help them get published any more than the great reviews of your novel would get you into medical school. Other items writers often include are positive comments from previous rejection letters, writing coaches and former teachers. These kinds of things are often skipped. However, if one of those former teachers is a well-known writer and has given you a positive prepublication endorsement, one that you have their permission to use on the book, this very well might make the editor predisposed to the book. For one thing, someone with authority has given your work their imprimatur; for another, the publisher knows that if they publish this book they will have a valuable selling tool to offer their sales representatives, who can use it when presenting to bookstores. But what if you don't know anybody famous? Have no previous publications? Then what you have is the work to speak for you – which puts you on the same playing field as all but the very small percentage of people whose names alone will get them published.

There are a number of resources for writers that are invaluable. See the Resources section for more details.

Always put a copyright slug at the end of whatever you send out. This gives you some legal protection. To register a copyright, you must ask for forms from your copyright or patent office. When you are published in a magazine or in book form, the publisher takes care of copyright registration for that issue or for your book. But always include your own slug on anything you send out.

Sometimes it is worthwhile to submit short pieces abroad, even if they have been published in your country first. You do not include an SASE but a self-addressed envelope with International Reply Coupons included, available at any post office. Canadian publication cannot duplicate publication in the U.S. The rights you give for U.S. publications are generally phrased as "North American first serial rights." That, naturally, includes Canada, and vice versa. If something is published first in a Canada, it cannot be submited in the U.S.

Publishing on-line is another way to get your work out, immediate but largely unprotected. You have to consider the pros and cons yourself. For both of us, our web pages are important and we put effort into them constantly. As often as time allows we post samples of our work, figuring that the offers for readings, workshops or lectures that come in, or the ability to reach a new reader, balance the risk of someone not bothering to buy books because they can get the work free on-line. As we write this, the world of on-line publishing has yet to make a definitive impression on the marketplace. In December, 2000, one prestigious internet industry research firm forecasted that by 2005 print-on-demand trade and text books and electronic books would account for revenues of $7.8 billion, 17.5 per cent of U.S. publishing industry revenues. But only about 3 per cent of this amount would be attributable to e-books. A study in October, 2000, reported that only 5 per cent of trade books were sold via on-line bookstores; a surprisingly small number in light of all the speculation concerning the impact of the web on publishing. While it is true that a few very popular authors were able to sell large numbers of the electronic versions of their work directly to the consumer, the web's economic impact is still yet to be felt for large publishers, independent presses and self-published authors alike. For now, if your work is on-line, or published in an electronic book, or print-on-demand format, getting the word out is still the key. If you are serious about building a name for yourself, you have to put effort into attracting readers. What that means is advertising the availability of your work everyplace you can think of, from the return address on your envelopes to the signature on your e-mail. There is no point here listing all the places to which you can submit your poems or stories or simply post them for discussion; no print publication can ever keep up with the ever-changing web. Theorizing about the implications of electronic publishing is fun but fruitless and reminiscent of the early 1980's when the most passionate conversations at literary cocktail parties and writers' conferences were about stand-alone word processors versus computers, Apple versus IBM, WordPerfect versus Word. As writers we have to be interested in putting out the best work we can, writing what is meaningful to people, no matter what technology we use to write or how it reaches people. The most important thing to know about on-line communications for writers today is that they will lose out if they are not flexible to change and on-line savvy.

Most communications with editors come through e-mail or fax, mostly the former. If you are not connected, you will be at a disadvantage. Some presses permit submissions via e-mail. An editor certainly wouldn't reject you if you weren't on-line, but should your work be accepted, you'd miss out on an intimacy with your editor born of hundreds of small decisions that take place in the publishing process. Although the product is ultimately a book, communication in publishing today, like all serious businesses, is largely conducted via e-mail. Those who are not on-line stand out as needlessly out of touch and out of date.

I should repeat that most magazines and small presses take far longer to read manuscripts than you would like to believe possible. Three to six months is not uncommon. Agents and editors at large publishing houses are not much faster. The submissions outnumber the people who read them by an exponential factor – and a great deal of the time and effort of those people is going into working with writers already signed on. When

I submit poems or stories and they come back, I reread them before sending them out again to see if I can make them stronger. However, I know that some of my best work was rejected again and again before it saw the light of print or electronic publication. If I believe in the work, I continue to believe in it whether the first ten places rejected it or not.

As a writer, the tendency is to see the publisher as someone who passes judgment on you. A more realistic image of small press editors as well as most agents and editors at large publishing houses is of an overburdened office worker desperately looking for a project they can love and champion, live with night and day for a year. They hope to find a work that come commercial or critical disappointment, they can be proud of. Think how many books you read in a year that you honestly feel this way about. Probably not many. When you read a book, especially if you've purchased it, you want to like it, but often you don't. So why imagine that an editor will like any book that happens to fall on the desk? Yes, there are issues of social class, sexism, age and race: book editors by and large are not representative of the population. There are always economic issues. Even non-profit small presses hope to publish books that will find a market. You may be rejected because the editor has no ability to empathize with the world or the characters you are writing about, but none of these issues is about you, the person who wrote the book. Editors do not know you, no matter how much of yourself you may have put into the work. Once a manuscript leaves your desk it has to make its own way. The editor who does not want to publish your book does not think of him or herself as a higher being than you any more than you think yourself a higher being than the author of some novel you don't like. If you can't grasp that, writing is always going to be fraught with disappointment. The writer's ability to accept rejection is as much a part of a writer's job as a quarterback's ability to withstand being knocked down. Sending the manuscript out again and again is as important as the writing itself. If you don't write it, it can't get published; but neither can it get published if it is not continually placed in front of as many editors as possible.

When you are sending around a manuscript and editors give you suggestions to revise it (but are not offering money to buy it), read their comments, take them seriously but with a grain of salt. Hardly anyone ever has the time to write a complete and well-thought-out critique. They may point out something that gave them pause, which may be the opposite of what another editor tells you. Or, it may be something they simply latch on to which gives them an excuse to reject you. A wise independent press editor once put it this way: The acquisitions function of an editor is not the same as the editorial function; even if it is the same editor. When reading for possible acquisition, an editor does not pay attention to fine details; it is possible too that if they did not accept it, they never read the whole book. Better to collect the comments of many editors before altering your vision. If four different editors tell you that Jim, the husband of your protagonist, comes off as a wooden stereotype, you may have work to do. If only one mentions it, it may be him, not Jim. I once destroyed a novel that kept almost making it with publishers. I would revise it after every rejection to please the last editor, and the next editor would want something entirely different. Finally my vision was lost and I had to put the novel aside for ten years before I could tackle it and do what I intended, and not what sixteen editors had said off the top of their heads while deciding not to take a chance on an unknown writer. The most honest rejection slip I ever received was from a West Coast poetry magazine. The editor wrote, "I like your poems, but I started this journal in order to publish my friends, and I don't publish people I don't know." I never forgot it and never held it against the editor – I often teach one of his poems in my poetry workshops.

Whether the editor took the trouble to write a critique of your work or not, it is rankly amateurish to reply – to argue, to denounce, to plead. You do NOT answer a rejection letter. You may kick the wall or yourself or stick pins in a clay doll, but you do not call up or write an answer.

Finally, what do you do if no one wants to publish your manuscript? There is probably not a writer you can name who does not have at least one book that never made it into print. Then there is the writer who suddenly bursts on the scene to spectacular reviews – whose first five books are in boxes on his shelf. John Gardner, when a novel was finally accepted, also had several others ready to go.

Often, the work that is most like last year's big hit finds its way into print, but the work that's most original is rejected time and again. Still, the question nags, how do I know it's good? How do I know I'm not crazy? Some people believe that everything they've written is a work of brilliance; some never have confidence in themselves. A writer who is wildly successful by anyone's standards told me, after a brilliant review in the *New York Times*, "I faked it." I said, "What do you mean?" He said, "I stole the whole plot from a novel that came out in the forties." I thought he was being falsely modest until he said a similar thing about his next book, also favorably reviewed. Then I understood, that's how he lives. He can't judge his own work. Many writers are blind to both their strengths and weaknesses. So the question nags. How do you know you're not crazy, that if no publishing company bites, the book is good enough to be published?

The answer may be that the question itself is not good enough. Libraries are full of books that some readers love and others despise. If you're serious about your work, if you've studied enough writing to feel that it stands up, if your readers' opinions are opposite those in your rejection letters, you may not want to wait for the publishing world to discover you. The cost of believing in your work is neither as expensive as a used car nor more vain than backing a business idea. You can publish your first book by yourself. Like James Joyce. And Hemingway. And Gertrude Stein. Like Richard Paul Evans who self-published *The Christmas Box* and then re-sold it to a large commercial press. If you believe it is vanity to publish yourself, then you probably believe that no one should go to college unless they get a scholarship. Or that it is vain for Stephen Spielberg to produce his own movies. Self-publishing involves a tremendous amount of work but there are many resources to help you. There's an entire subculture of one- and two-book publishers who are passionate about the subject and more than willing to act as mentors. Moreover, there are many choices. You can print actual books or print-on-demand, electronic books or those appearing on websites. The Publishers Marketing Association, with 3400 members, is the largest book publishing trade association in the world. It offers invaluable information and marketing clout to its members, both on-line and through seminars. On its website (http://www.pma-online.org) you can access more up-to-date information about the practical aspects of seeing your work through to print and distribution than we can begin even to mention in this book. If you believe in your work, there are more ways of getting it out to the world than at any time in history.

The old models, those of the pained, solitary genius creating in a vacuum and mailing their book off to a gentleman publisher, are largely dead. The writer today is an entrepreneur, a person who believes in herself and backs up that belief by publicizing, marketing and if necessary financing the work. Some of today's best-selling writers are on the road with every book (and have made themselves best-selling writers by doing so). While there are those who are too timid to read to an audience, too proud to tour, too jaded to answer the mundane questions of interviewers, they demur at their own risk. The field is too crowded. With 60,000 titles published every year in the U.S. alone, the writer who holds back is the writer who is forgotten. There are important people to meet when you hit the trail to push your work: other writers who will trade battle stories and connections, bookstore owners and librarians who will buy your work, fans who will remember you the next time around. Seeking the information to publish yourself opens you to an on-line world of thousands of other writers whose experiences may be similar to your own. Marketing develops community. Once again, there are more ways of getting your work out to the world than at any time in history, but you must change your notion of the writer as a solitary creator to that of a creative entrepreneur. Once the work out there, you have to draw people to it.

13

Frequently Answered Questions

A T THE END OF EVERY workshop, we invite questions. Sometimes the same questions are repeated again and again in slightly different form by many people, which leads us to believe that either they didn't like the answers the first time, or that these were the questions they really came to the workshop to get answered. It doesn't surprise us that we are also told that other workshop leaders give different answers to the same questions. Writers, like critics, are full of prejudices. We freely admit that these are our opinions. Sometimes we don't even agree with each other.

1. Do I Need an Agent?

You will if you want to be published by a large mainstream publishing company. Good agents know who is open to publishing what kinds of work; who at the large companies have the power to make decisions. Good agents make it their business to keep their ears open to changes in the publishing business and to make connections with editors. Editors are extremely busy, more so as bottom line demands have cut staffing and they are responsible for many additional tasks. Many editors today rely on agents to cull through literary magazines, visit writers' conferences and keep abreast of cultural trends. Some agents make it their business to discover talent and cultivate it; some agents are hands-on editors.

We've known unrepresented writers who have gotten their work read by editors at the large publishing houses as a result of some connection (an established writer or a relative) but when the editors were ready to make an offer, they advised the writers to find a literary agent (who, with a contract pending, was obviously easier to engage). Publishing contracts with large, and increasingly with independent and university publishing houses, can be complex, involving the distribution of foreign, translation, theatrical, electronic rights and many other provisions including warranties, indemnities, royalties and accounting, discontinuance of publication, etc. Some agents are open to submitting to smaller presses once they feel they have exhausted their possibilities with the large houses, some are not. When Ira could not get *The Kitchen Man* published, he sent it to independent presses himself – and suffered a standard not very good contract. When the same thing happened with his next novel, *Going Public*, his new agent at one of New York's largest literary agencies continued to represent the book because, even though no real money was forthcoming, she understood that once in print, she could negotiate paperback, foreign and theatrical rights. It is possible to pay an agent or a lawyer a fee to look over your contract if you don't have an agent representing you. There are also some excellent books on the market that address publishing contracts. But while most independent presses will read work that is submitted directly by the writer, it is much more difficult to get a serious reading with a large press editor. One last thing worth mentioning is that some inexperienced writers feel that once they have an agent, a big agent who represents big name talents, the road to success is paved. Unfortunately, while an attachment to such an agent may initially give your work some cachet, get it into the hands of editors higher up on the food chain, and get you a quicker reading, it is ultimately the work that counts. A less glitzy agent who believes in your talent in the long run is probably a better bet. However, if you are writing poetry or literary fiction, you may want to go to a small press. In that case, an agent is no advantage in getting published.

2. How Do I Get an Agent?

There are a number of books available that list agents' names and specialties, some of the better ones written by agents themselves. A simple search for "literary agents" on the internet will yield well over a hundred sources. See Resources for more information. We'd like to emphasize the importance of a face-to-face meeting with the agent before you make your final decision. There is often a chemistry involved between you and an agent and that is difficult to determine without a meeting. All new clients are treated well, and why not? You are brimming with potential. It is only after the book is returned a few times that the relationship can be truthfully evaluated. Is the agent giving up on you? Is she returning your calls? Does she sound discouraged on the telephone, or worse, is she beginning to blame you for the failure of your book to find a publisher? While an initial visit can't answer these questions, you can get an inkling of what the future might hold. You can observe them in action. Do they speak dismissively to people on the telephone? Ira once had a meeting with an agent who put him on an extension phone and allowed him to listen as the agent dealt with a small publisher condescendingly. Although he felt like an insider at the moment, it didn't take him long to realize that this agent might very well treat him or his publisher like this one day.

Does their office seem disorganized? Are they forthcoming with the list of clients they represent? Are they open to considering independent presses? Make it a point to visit a few potential agents. Just a half-hour chat – an office visit may be better than lunch; you can observe them at work – can hint about your potential relationship later on.

3. Are Agents in Big Cities Better than those Out of Town?

Many writers do prefer to be represented by an agent with a big city office (or those located in a media center) because it is felt that these agents are more likely to be in-the-loop, or industry insiders. But there are a growing number of good agents who are located in cities around the country who specialize in representing writers from their regions, and others who have worked many years in big city publishing and, having developed their contacts, have set up shop in places which can afford them another lifestyle. Still, there are changes taking place in publishing all the time and you should ask any potential agent how they manage to stay current. Some are on the phone all day every day and manage their contacts with editors on a regular basis. Not all publishers, certainly not independent and university presses, are located in big cities. But it is easy for someone to call themselves a literary agent no matter where they live. Always ask the agent to tell you who they represent and what they have sold recently – they're usually proud of this. Determine if they are members of an association of author's representatives. Never pay an agent for reading your work, even if they tell you they will reimburse you with the proceeds of your first sale. The job of agents is to read the work of writers. If they take you on, they will attach fifteen per cent of everything of yours that they sell. This is how they earn their money. While you may be billed for postage, copying, bank fees, etc., you are not responsible for paying for their reading time.

4. Publishers Take So Long, Can I Make Multiple Submissions?

This is a question that, as writers and publishers, we fall on both sides of, and can probably be answered best by telling two stories. We were reading a first novel that needed work but one that had great potential. Before we committed to it, we needed to know if the writer was willing to make the many changes necessary. But of course, the writer wanted specifics. We re-read the manuscript at a great expense of time, detailing those changes. Finally, we heard back from the writer. Sorry, he was no longer interested in us. The book had been on submission to another press, which liked it as it was. This was, of course, our own fault and the writer's choice, but we felt burned nonetheless, in light of all the time and free advice expended.

Now for the writer's side of the story. After I had spent two years attempting to get *The Kitchen Man* published in New York, I sent the novel out to two small presses. When it was accepted by one, I took the offer immediately and wrote a courteous note to the other press, stating (untruthfully) that the Crossing Press editor had heard me read at a library and offered me a contract on the spot. I heard nothing back from that other press. Three years later, when I was submitting my next novel *Going Public*, I received the following note: "Dear Mr. Wood, Some years ago you submitted *The Kitchen Man* to us and withdrew it while we were in the middle of reading it. Good luck with your *Going Public* elsewhere." Did I get arrested? No. Was my career over? Of course not. There are no laws saying you can't multiply submit, even if the press explicitly asks you not to. But small presses have long memories and it's always been my habit to attempt to curry friends in the very small world of publishing rather than enemies.

5. Isn't It Better to be Published by a Large Publisher than a Small Press?

If you are looking for a sizable advance against royalties, you should indeed try to place your book with a large publisher. If the publisher feels the book has big commercial potential, if their sales force is able to sell-in a substantial number of copies to bookstores (that is, get a large advance order), the big corporate-owned publisher may assign the book a large marketing budget. It may decide to place ads in national newspapers and magazines. It may send you on tour, pay the promotional fees required by chain bookstores to insure prominent shelf and catalog placement and attempt to arrange national talk show interviews for you. You need to be aware, however, that the size, famous name and wealth of a publisher, no matter how many books it has on the best-seller lists, is no guarantee that your book will get that treatment. A large publisher publishes a large number of books. They cannot possibly allot a huge marketing budget to each one. While most large publishers are very good at sending out review copies, and while book review editors might have a certain prejudice for the titles published by them, being published by a big city press is no guarantee of being reviewed. Space for book reviews in newspapers is extremely tight. Many writers are surprised that a publisher would fork out what seems like a very sizable advance and not back up that advance with marketing support. But again, the large publisher has a lot of titles to market and will throw its support behind those books that have gotten the really big advances (after all, it's a bigger investment to protect), those that have had a terrific sell-in (it makes more sense to support books that are in the stores than the warehouse) and those sleepers that come along and catch fire. According to the "Report to the Authors Guild Midlist Books Study Committee" by David D. Kirkpatrick, the average literary book gets less than $5,000 of total marketing support by a conglomerate-owned publisher, "but just to get a book put on a table at the front of the store in one of the chains can cost $10,000." Writers are also devastated when their books go out of print, a situation that is quite common because large publishers, required by their conglomerate owners to watch the bottom line, have to pay taxes on their inventory. If a book is not selling at certain rate, it will be shredded.

Independent, not-for-profit presses tend to keep books in print for a very long time, and even small presses that don't have not-for-profit status keep enough copies on-hand to make it available for sale years after publication, when a writer's reputation has grown and she is more likely to be asked to do readings, workshops, etc. These presses tend to publish far fewer books a season, so every title gets more of the publicist's time, if admittedly a smaller budget. Some small presses do send writers on tour and may have excellent contacts with the media. Some small presses are also very good at getting books reviewed. It is not uncommon for a dogged and enthusiastic publicist with unconventional marketing ideas to obtain more visibility for a book than a large and busy publicity department.

6. How Much Money Do Writers Make?

At a lecture in Flagstaff, Arizona, some years ago, Toni Morrison was asked, "What advice would you give a young person who wants to be a writer?" Without a second thought, the Nobel laureate and best-selling author answered something akin to, Don't quit your day job. Toni Morrison was writing brilliant novels long before they began to appear on the best-seller lists. While raising two children, she worked for many years as an editor at Random House, where she not only had to juggle her writing, her career and her family life, but observed countless writers who had to do so as well. I would date it to be some time in the eighties, but it may have been long before, that the notion of the writer's life became confused with that of the screenwriter's life; that is, that the definition of the "successful" writer was one who was rich instead of widely read. In earlier decades, writers were assumed to be intellectuals rather than personalities; renegades as opposed to millionaires. People might dismiss your latest book by saying, "Never heard of it," but rarely by asking, "Is it a best-seller?" as if to insinuate that if it is not, it isn't worth mentioning. Only a very small percentage of writers reach the best-seller lists. Because there are so many titles printed every year, readers tend to opt for the books by authors they are familiar with as well as books heavily advertised by the chain bookstores. A perusal of the best-seller lists will yield the same names year after year. So the rich writers are getting richer and the poor. . . well, you know how it goes. Which is not to say there aren't surprises. New people break in all the time. Publishers have not stopped publishing literary books and in fact shelf space for them, as a result of the proliferation of chain mega-stores, has increased. It's just that it's getting almost impossible for them to get noticed. In his "Report to the Authors Guild Midlist Books Study Committee" Kirkpatrick gives an example of "the best possible outcome for a midlist author." He sites the example of David Foster Wallace's novel *Infinite Jest*, which sold 30,000 copies in hardcover, and 60,000 in paperback. Mr. Wallace received an $85,000 advance from his publisher, Little Brown (after his agent's 15 per cent commission), and another $42,500 in royalties, totaling $127,500. The book took him five years to write. You do the math. The report sums it up: "Writing books is a losing proposition financially for most writers. Serious authorship is not now and has never been self-supporting, except in a rare handful of cases." In 1981, the Authors Guild Foundation commissioned a report on authors' incomes from the Center for Social Science at Columbia University, which found that the median income for an American writer is about $5,000. According to Mr. Kirkpatrick's informative study, copyright, 2000, "That figure has probably not changed substantially." Don't quit your day job.

7. You Mentioned that You Don't Consider it "Vanity" to Publish Yourself. What then Constitutes a Vanity Publisher?

Even in the very difficult publishing environment we've mentioned, there are many opportunities for writers, especially with publishers who are creative, willing to look at new models. Electronic publishing is the most often mentioned model today because an e-book is inexpensive to produce, easy to update, and does not present the costly problems of a paper-book inventory so writing can theoretically remain in print indefinitely. But few publications review e-books, and they have had disappointing sales. Moreover, the devices needed to read them are clunky and expensive. A more promising model might prove to be print-on-demand, in which a publisher will literally print a book when it is ordered or print a small number to satisfy anticipated demand.

Some paper-and-ink publishers, as well as publishers who work with the new technologies mentioned above, invite authors to subsidize the production of their own books and here the author has to be especially careful. Costs can be high; some that I've heard quoted almost double that of producing the book yourself. But this estimate may cover marketing. Marketing is the key. If the publisher is going to produce an agreed upon number of books, including bound galleys which are submitted for review, warehouse the book (or print it on demand), include it in their catalog, make it available through national wholesalers as well as the on-line booksellers, then the money you spend might be seen as an investment in your work and your writing career. I would contrast this with what has been known as a vanity publisher, who will produce (or promise to produce) an agreed upon number of copies, send you your share, and let the rest rot in their warehouse. Sometimes they never print the books that are supposed to be in the warehouse. The difference, of course, is the commitment to get the work out to the reading public. An honest subsidy publisher will treat your book like any other publishing house. A vanity publisher will ship you a box of books. In spite of their promises, that is all you will get.

Appendix I

Excerpted from *The Kitchen Man*, as referred to in Chapter 10

I am a soldier in the service of the appetites of the rich, a waiter at Les Nieges d'Antan. The Snows of Yesterday, the finest restaurant north of New York City, a number one choice in the haute cuisine category of every magazine in which we advertise.

I assume a position of parade rest amid the commingling aromas of pipe smoke and fresh cut flowers. Vowels of contentment. . . aahhhhh. . . announce the presentation of a meal; bedroom groans – Ooh, no! I can't stand it, stop! – greet the squeaking wheels of the dessert cart. Saturday evening, we have been fully booked since Tuesday, and all goes according to meticulous plan.

Until I am called to the telephone.

"It's your mother." She announces herself like the finance company, to get the bad news over with, as if she's a burden.

"Mom, how are you?"

"What do you care?"

"I do care. I love you."

"No, you don't."

Understand, this can go on for half an hour. I do, you don't. I do, you don't. My mother's keenest pleasure is the affirmation of other people. To that end she demeans herself to everyone. The dentist. The dry cleaning man. The plumber. Lady, you need a new hot water heater. It's my fault. No Lady, it's not. It is. It's not. It is. What does he care at sixty dollars an hour? The only way to stop it is to wait, pause; you don't disagree with her, she can't disagree with you. "So," finally she goes on, "how do you like your new apartment?"

"We love it, as soon as we're settled you'll have to come over."

"You wish I never called, don't you?"

"Why do you say that? Of course I don't."

"You do."

"I don't."

Pause.

"So, Gabriel, when are we going to see you the parents who love you so much?"

"Tell you what, call me at my new number. Tomorrow, in the afternoon and we'll make a date."

"I'd rather call you at the restaurant."

At this moment thirty customers are staring at my back, squirming, yawning, dying for another cup of coffee. Some raise one finger to get my attention – very continental. Some smile, the friendly approach. Some brood, Wait until you see your check, Jerk. "It's not good to call me here, Mom."

"You call me back then, darling."

"Why, what's the matter? Why can't you call me at home?"

"I'd rather not, that's all. You know me. What if *she* answers?"

She is an Obie Award winning playwright, a professor of theater. *She* is the person I live with, the person I love.

"The woman, Gabriel."

"Her name is Cynthia."

"Very nice. But I'd feel funny. So you call me, okay?"

"Mom, what's the matter with you?"

"I don't know if you want me to be honest or not?" Honest, in my family, is synonymous with vicious. To be open with each other is to attack, to unload every unkind, sordid impression. To protect yourself in my family you have to say, "please don't be honest," which undermines the very notion of family and makes you feel like a coward. "To be honest," my mother continues, "she's practically my age."

This is not true. Cynthia is ten years older than me. "And she's practically my wife."

"Gabriel, I don't expect you to understand. You will when you get older."

My mother is a sixty-seven-year-old size five petite, an anorexic Madame Bovary, in love with romance, at war with aging. My mother starved and drugged me until I was twelve years old. Philip Roth had nothing to complain about.

I read about Sophie Portnoy. I dreamed about Sophie Portnoy, balabusta, matriarch, kitchen witch. Arms soft as overripe honeydew folded over a flower print dress, standing above her ungrateful Alex begging him to eat, rooting for his appetite like a ticket holder at a horse race. Please, Darling, the crisp roast potatoes and the warm apple sauce. The sweet nutty tsimmis and the flanken. The way you like it. Try, Precious. Honeycake for dessert. Raspberry sherbet, too, for my hungry boy.

My mother weighed every item she served me on a plastic scale. She had a local handyman drill a padlock on the refrigerator door. She emptied my pockets for loose change before I left the house and cruised the shopping plaza because a neighbor kid told her I sometimes bought a knish and devoured it by the dumpster in back of the deli. She ran her fingers around the waist band of my pants to make sure they were not tightening (to this day I opt to drip rather than tumble dry, having more than once been the innocent victim of shrinkage). She clicked her tongue in disgust when the clothing salesman led us past the regular sizes to the elephant tent of the children's wear department: the table marked Huskies.

I was weighed four times a week, always showing far above the Metropolitan Life Average Weight for Children (of India? I wondered) and driven bi-monthly to a diet doctor whose lunch clung to his mustache, who pinched my flesh blue and prescribed amphetamines. Before every meal I choked down a black pill whose street value today is six dollars. My hands shook. My stomach was an express elevator. I was a chronic insomniac at ten years old. Alex Portnoy locked himself in the bathroom and wacked himself silly. With so much speed in me I couldn't even get it up.

But I couldn't blame her, not then, not now. I was grown before my time – tall and broad, the kids called me Haystacks, after a TV wrestler who was buried in a piano crate – and she never grew up. A bobby soxer at thirty, adulthood took her by surprise. Lost in some Andrew's Sisters movie she hummed "Mares eat oats and lambs eat oats" as she primped in her bedroom for hours, discarding blouses, trying lipsticks, just to walk down to Shirley Avenue for milk and cold cuts. She batted her eyes at every man on every corner and giggled every time the greasy butcher rolled his toothpick on his tongue and said, "You want some meat today?" But I blew it for her. A baby boomer stuffed with the seven basic food groups I exceeded all genetic expectations. I was my grandfather's pride, a brick shit house, second generation grown weed-wild. But she couldn't be the neighborhood flirt with an enormous son in tow.

She was my confidant; I, her only friend. Pals, we shopped together, sipped lemon Tabs, practiced the fox trot and the lindy my father was always too tired to learn. At ten years old I knew all about Howard, the man she could have married, who had acne pimples big as candy corn, but who would have made us rich. I knew she hated her big nose, that it kept her from being beautiful, that she saved quarters and nickels in a jar to have it fixed. Together we sang the song she once wrote that was as good as any on the radio. Silently we wished that one day the car would not turn into the driveway at six o'clock, that one day my father would not clop up the stairs and throw his business problems on the couch with the evening *Post*. Silently we wished to go off, mother and son, the bobby soxer and the brick shit house, in search of a contract for her song, in search of Howard, and a nose job.

"Mom, I want you to meet Cynthia. I want us all to have supper together, I want – "

"Your father and I want to see our son, Gabriel. You don't have to drag along some stranger just because we're too boring to take up your precious time."

"Who said that? I didn't say you were too boring."

"But we are."

"You're not."

"We are."

Tonight we're meeting my parents at a Chinese restaurant: their choice. Then we're all four going to a performance of Cynthia's play: my choice. They were scared. They've never been to the theater. They tried to beg out but I held firm. If we're ever going to be close again we have to bust out of our tired old patterns.

"Jesus Christ." Wearing black pants and a black shirt I am sucking in my stomach in front of the hallway mirror. "I look as fat as a pig."

"Fat?" Cynthia is applying her makeup in the bedroom. "You've been starving yourself for two days and I'm warning you, Gabriel, Chinese food is full of MSG and you're going to get sick."

This brings me to the door. "Promise me. *Promise me* you're not going to start in front of my parents with the MSG in the food."

"What, start? You don't have a body like everybody else? MSG on an empty stomach doesn't make you sick?"

"Please?" I am not above getting down on my knees. "For me. Just this once. Don't haggle about the chemicals in the food. My parents will not understand. They simply will not understand."

"Then why in the world are we eating Chinese food when you knew you were going to starve yourself beforehand?"

"Because my father won't eat anything else." This is a fact. At Gettysburg, at Fort Ticonderoga, at Valley Forge, wherever we went on vacation, my father would never eat supper anywhere but at a Chinese restaurant. In Williamsburg, Virginia, my baby sister yowling with hunger, we drove two hours to find a place staffed by blond William and Mary students in magenta luau shirts. Ditto Amish country. Red checker table cloths. Soy sauce in cellophane packets. You know you're in trouble when the waiter comes to your table with bread and butter in a wicker basket. "And just ignore it when my father starts to speak Chinese."

Cynthia is suddenly impressed. "You never told me your father speaks Chinese."

"He doesn't. So I beg you. Please. Ignore it."

Jimmy Lee's Happy Talk Lounge, Dad's favorite restaurant, is two-thirds empty. My parents are sitting in a corner booth, under a canopy of bamboo and thatch, next to a plastic Mugo pine. The ashtray is overfull. There are two highballs in front of Mom, two cokes in front of Dad. He never drinks. When Mom sees us she pops the pill she's been clutching, bolts down whatever is left in her glass, and waves. Toodle—oo. Dad stands.

I take one last look at Cynthia in her red crepe suit, elegant enough to please my mother, low-cut enough to interest Dad. Knowing my father has a sweet tooth she baked brownies for him last night; knowing my mother is phobic about long hair, Cyn trimmed hers two inches.

"Gabriel, oh, Gabriel." Mom is still a perfect size five, still consumes no solid food except Sarah Lee cake. Her every vertebrae is as distinct as a swollen knuckle and as I envelop her in a welcoming hug I imagine a skeleton shellacked with hair spray.

"My Gabey," Dad says as we paddle each other on the back. He is a tall man for his generation, with a chest like an oak wine cask and a round fluid middle. His name is Sam, nicknamed Samson, all his life likened to an ox. "Gabey, Gabey," he sighs, proud. "How's your car?"

Mom steps back to view me at arm's length. Her hair is red now. It was blond before the summer. "You look gorgeous. Look at that handsome face. So you have a belly," she goes straight for the bulge over my belt and twists it like challah dough. "When you get older everybody gets a belly."

"Except for Doctor Pincus. Doctor Pincus has no belly," Dad says.

My mother freezes. Her eyes squint warning. "Don't start."

"Oh, svelte Doctor Pincus with his little mustache. He looks like David Niven your mother says."

"He's a cultured, educated man, Sam".

"He's a fairy."

"This is a poor man whose wife passed away a year ago. According to your father he's beating down my door. He's not looking for a woman of sixty-seven, believe me. Nobody's looking for a woman of sixty-seven."

They moved to their present house during my first year away at college. Vaguely, I recall a sign in front of a split-level across the street: I. G. Pincus, optometrist. "He told me my wife had the eyes of a forty-year-old woman."

My mother lights up. "When did he say that?"

"I almost sent him to the moon." Dad balls his fist. "He should talk about my wife's eyes."

I smile at Cynthia, a sad but victorious, "I told you so." For months Cynthia thought I was keeping her from meeting my parents because I was ashamed of her. Now, ignored, foil-wrapped gift in hand, she can observe them for herself as they make the entire world their stage. Perhaps in another life they would have become the Lunts.

"Mom, I'd like you to meet –"

"Just a minute, Gabriel. When did Doctor Pincus say that, Sam? I want to know."

"Mom, this is Cynthia."

"Yes, darling, of course, yes." My mother smiles but her eyes do not leave my father's. She kisses Cynthia's cheek. "Hello, hello, Cynthia. Did Gabriel tell you I saw one of your books in the library? I was so proud.

But if you want me to be honest, I asked my friends and nobody's ever heard of you."

"It's Doctor Pincus who's never heard of you," Dad says.

There is nothing left to do but eat. Mom seats us. "Sam and Gabe, there. Cynthia and I, here. And you two take these." Mom pushes the little wooden bowl of crispy noodles to our side of the table. "We certainly don't need these, do we?" Mom says to Cynthia. "Not at our age."

"Ah, Gabey, Gabey," Dad sighs. He squeezes my knee. "My first and only son. You look terrific." He snaps his fingers. "Waiter!"

I want to evaporate. I want to disappear. If anyone in my restaurant snaps his fingers for my attention, I ignore him. The waiters here do, too.

"Chop Chop! Ching Low!" Dad calls.

"Pop," I say gently. "Maybe if you don't make fun of their language. Maybe if you spoke to them with a little respect."

"Oh, I see, I see." Dad slides, huffing, out of the booth. He stands next to the table and bows to a passing waiter. "Oh, excuse me, kind sir. Excuse me for troubling you. But if you do not mind the inconvenience, would you deign to honor us by gracing our table with an order of egg rolls?"

I glance at Cynthia for help, acknowledgement, anything, but my mother is commanding her complete attention. ". . . and Doctor Pincus says I should not be ashamed to admit that I've had a hysterectomy. It's not uncommon for a woman our age, right?"

I eat and I eat. I cannot hear their voices when I eat. The rice steams in its little bowl, sticky as a snowball, the mustard burns my sinus clear, the charred flesh of the pink sparerib flakes on my fingertips as the hot juice runs down my chin. I eat it all, everything. I refill my plate with the sweet and sour gravy, the shredded mu shu pork, the soggy mattress of egg fu yung, the crunchy water chestnuts.

I eat and I grow young, a child again at my parents' table. I eat and watch them, huge as dinosaurs, knocking each other over with the thunderous wallop of their scaly tails. I eat now as I ate then, compulsively chewing, swallowing, trying not hear my mother screaming at my father he was too fat to sleep with. I eat now as I ate then, as my mother sobbed through our entire Thanksgiving dinner, her food untouched, her tears falling into her cranberry sauce and making it run in thin maroon rivers.

I ate as my mother watched the clock and my father slept off his depression, Friday night to Monday morning, awakening only for trips to the bathroom, fingers digging into the crotch of his wrinkled boxer shorts.

"Look at him eat with chopsticks," my father says with pride. It is the small changes he notices, the gestures acquired away from home. I'll order an after supper eau de vie, suggest we watch Masterpiece Theater instead of Sunday Night Football. The small things, each one a wave taking me farther out to sea. "Gabey, Gabey," he shakes my shoulder with love. "How's your car?" It is only when I visit my father that I appreciate engine failure.

"Car's fine, Pop."

"You got enough money, Gabey?" Dad whispers. "You had to bake the brownies, you couldn't buy them?"

"I'm working. No complaints." I take more rice, more mu shu pork.

"How come we never see you? You don't love us anymore, Gabey?"

"Of course I love you, Daddy." One more egg roll. One more butterfly shrimp. A last ladle of Five Happiness chicken.

"Naw," my father sighs, "you don't love us."

"But I do."

"You don't."

"I do."

"You don't."

Pause.

Her food untouched, glazed and reflecting the yellow light of the Chinese lanterns, my other shakes her head and sighs. "You don't talk to us anymore. Not like you used to."

I am having momentary difficulty catching my breath. "Sure I talk to you."

"Oh, you tell us all the time what's good. Everything is fine. You never talk to us like your sister does. You never tell us what's really on your mind."

I am slightly nauseous now. It comes in waves. One minute I feel feverish and about to fall over, the next I start to shiver. No, I don't talk to them now, I don't try to communicate. I blather on like a happy idiot, like an AM disc jockey. The last time I tried to talk honestly, to help them with their problems, I sat my mom down on the couch and held her. My voice trembled. She was crying. She hated living with him, she said, she cursed the day they were married. "Mama, if you are in so much pain, maybe you should separate for a while."

That evening my father called me at my apartment. "So you told your mother to leave me, you little prick?"

All sound is muted. All lights in blur. I hear Cynthia defending me. I hear her ask my mother why only negative feelings are real ones.

"You don't understand," my mother says with contempt. "You have children and they become strangers and it hurts."

"But I do understand," Cynthia says. "I do have children."

"So you're a success, we're failures," my mother says.

"You're not."

"We are."

"You're not."

"We are."

I have never been so hungry. I am eating the last of the white rice and lobster sauce. I scrape the soggy water chestnuts from my mother's plate.

"Gabe, maybe you should slow down a bit," Cynthia reaches for my wrist.

"Let him live." My father shows his teeth. "Eat, Gabey, eat. It's good here, huh? Remember we used to be so close? We ate out every Sunday. We went on trips together. Remember we went to the Amish country? Oh, we found a good restaurant there."

My throat is dry, so dry I can only nod. I reach for my water glass, swallow it all, then Cynthia's.

"Remember the trip we took to Washington?" Dad continues.

On that particular excursion my father was mute for seven and a half hours, fuming anger like a toaster with crust jammed against its heating coil. Finally exploding, on the sixteen lane highway that rings the capital, he said he was only on this goddamned trip because he'd never hear the end of it from my mother if he didn't spend his only vacation schlepping his kids to Washington, D.C. So leave! Go home! My mother wailed. She grabbed at the wheel. He shoved her away. We swerved off the road and my sister lost three teeth when her head rammed sideways into the ashtray.

"We had some good times, huh, Gabey?"

"Leave him, Sam," my mother says. "They get older they go off. They forget all the love."

"Want some dessert, Gabey? Hey, boy! Chop Chop!"

I breathe deeply, I steady myself. When the dizziness passes I will walk calmly to the men's room.

"How about ice cream, Gabey?" Dad says when the waiter arrives. "What you got? Van—ee—ra? Choc—rit? Slaw—belly?"

"Maybe he's eaten enough," Cynthia says.

"Leave him be, let him be a man." Dad burps, one of those intentionally loud, smelly burps, designed to shock.

"Sam!" my mother scolds him.

"So sorry, miss," my father bows to Cynthia. "You're an intellectual, I'm sorry. Maybe you never heard a burp before."

I am on my feet, not aware of having planned to stand up, but lurching to the door for air.

"It's the MSG, the chemicals," Cynthia says.

"Oh, the chemicals, pardon me," Dad says. "We should have eaten health food."

"Go to him, darling, take care of him," I hear my mother say to Cynthia. "Go!"

In the parking lot I stand spread-eagle over the trunk of my car. Cynthia paces, alternately caressing me, stroking my back, wiping my forehead; alternately raging. "What kind of idiot doesn't eat for two days and then poisons himself?"

"I was trying to look nice, to please them, to make them happy."

"But they are happy."

"They're miserable."

"But that's it, Gabriel, don't you see? They're happy being miserable."

"You wouldn't say that if they were your parents. I can change them, Cynthia. *We* can, together. By taking their minds off their own problems and helping them focus on the world. It's a slow process, I know. Tonight, the play. Next week something else. They're asking for help, don't you see? Who in the world wants to be miserable?"

My mother lights a fresh cigarette from the one in her mouth when she sees us come in. Dad is finishing a dish of chocolate ice cream. "Feel better, darling?" My mother reaches for my forehead. "You should go home and lie down."

"You should, Gabey. We're beat, too. We're just going to go back to the house and watch TV."

"But Cynthia's play. . ."

"We wouldn't like it, darling."

"But you don't know that."

"We're too old, Gabey. Your father likes to go to bed early. I like my coffee and cake. We're just that way."

On the way out the waiter stops me, not to thank me for the five dollars he saw me add to my father's tip, but to hand me the foil-wrapped brownies dad left in the booth.

Appendix II

Recommended Books

In our tradition, there is a story often told about the great sage, Rabbi Hillel. A Roman soldier, taunting him, said he must recite the entire Torah while standing on one foot. Hillel thought for a moment, standing with difficulty, for he was an old man. "That which is hateful to you, do not do to your neighbor," he said. "That is the whole Torah; the rest is commentary."

Okay, maybe you've read this entire book cover to cover. Or maybe you read writing books the way you read mysteries, so you skipped to the end. Maybe you're standing in a bookstore right now and are trying to see what tips you can pick up without buying the book at all. No matter. We're going to sum up the entire book, everything we have to say about how to learn to write in one sentence, like Rabbi Hillel:

If You Want To Be a Writer, Be a Reader.

That's it. That's the whole deal. As we said back in Chapter One, if you want to write memoirs, read one hundred of them. Figure out how other writers have avoided making themselves victims or failed to; figure out how other writers with great accomplishments in their middle age managed to solve the problem of keeping readers hooked while recounting a relatively uneventful childhood. If you want to write suspense novels, read all the thrillers you can find and pay attention to how these writers end one chapter to build anticipation for the next, or drop hints early on that will figure into the plot later. Or fail to. Bad writing can be as instructive as successful writing.

Just because you've been reading since you were five does not mean, no matter how interesting your life, that you can write about it in an interesting way. We do not suggest reading books like this one in hopes of finding a formula, but books in which other writers have managed to overcome the same problems of craft that you will inevitably face. *If you want to write, read.* The rest is commentary.

Here are some books you may find useful:

Allison, Dorothy.	*Bastard Out of Carolina*. Dutton, 1992.
Alvarez, Julia.	*Yo!* Algonquin, 1997.
	In the Name of Salome. Algonquin, 2000.
Asaro, Catherine.	*The Last Hawk*. St. Martins Press, 1998.
Angelou, Maya.	*Singin' and Swingin' and Getting' Merry Like Christmas*. Random House, 1976. Memoir.
	All God's Children Need Traveling Shoes. Vintage Books, 1991. Memoir.
	I Know why the Caged Bird Sings. Random House, 1970. Memoir.
Atwood, Margaret.	*Surfacing*. Simon & Schuster, 1972.
Ballard, J.G.	*Empire of the Sun*. Pocketbooks, 1985. Memoir.
Barington, Judith.	*Lifesaving*. Eighth Mountain Press, 2000. Memoir.
Bragg, Rich.	*All Over But the Shoutin'*. Pantheon, 1997. Memoir.
Brecht, Bertold.	*Three Penny Opera*. Arcade, 1995.
	Threepennny Novel. (Out of Print).
Brontë, Charlotte.	*Jane Eyre*. Penguin Books, 1984.
Brownmiller, Susan.	*In Our Time: Memoir of a Revolution*. Dial Press, 1999. Memoir.
Burke, James Lee.	*Burning Angel*. Hyperion, 1985.
Casella, Casare, (with Eileen Daspin).	*Diary of a Tuscan Chef*. Doubleday, 1998. Memoir.
Chabon, Michael.	*Mysteries of Pittsburgh*. Morrow, 1988.
	Werewolves in Their Youth. Random House. 1999.
Chaucer.	*Canterbury Tales*. Bantam, 1982.
Conrad, Joseph.	*Heart of Darkness*. Penguin, 1999.
	Lord Jim. Oxford University Press, 2000.
Danticat, Edwidge.	*Krik? Krok!* Random House, 1996.
De Beauvoir, Simone.	*Memoirs of a Dutiful Daughter*. Harper, 1974. Memoir.
	The Prime of Life. Marlowe & Co. 1994. Memoir.
	Force of Circumstance. Marlowe & Co. 1994. Memoir.
	The Coming of Age. Norton, 1996. Memoir.
	Adieux. Pantheon Books, 1984. Memoir.
	America Day by Day. University of California Press, 2000.
Delany, Samuel.	*Stars in My Pocket Like Grains of Sand*. Bantam, 1984.
	Triton. Bantam, 1984.
Dinesen, Isaak.	*Out of Africa*. Modern Library, 1992. Memoir.
Doctorow, E.L.	*Ragtime*. Random House, 1975.
	Loon Lake. Bantam, 1981.
Dos Passos, John.	*U.S.A.* (Trilogy). Library of America, 1996.

Dunnett, Dorothy.	*The Game of Kings.* Vintage, 1997. (Or any of the books in the *Lymond Chronicle* Series.)
Evans, Richard Paul.	*The Christmas Box.* Simon & Schuster, 1995.
Eve, Nomi.	*The Family Orchard.* Knopf, 2000.
Faulkner, William.	*Sanctuary.* Library of America, 1985.
Ferrell, Carolyn.	*Don't Erase Me.* Houghton Mifflin, 1997.
Finney, Patricia.	*Firedrake's Eye.* Picador, 1992.
Fisher, M.F.K.	A *Cordial Water.* North Point Press, 1981. Memoir. *The Gastronomical Me.* North Point Press, 1989. Memoir.
Fitzgerald, F. Scott.	*The Great Gatsby.* Scribner, 1995. *Tender Is the Night.* Scribner, 1996.
Flanagan, Mary.	"Cream Sauce." In *Bad Girls* (stories), Atheneum, 1985.
Fowles, John.	*The Collector.* Little Brown, 1963. The French Lieutenant's Woman. Little Brown, 1969.
Frank, Anne.	*The Diary of Anne Frank.* Doubleday, 1952. Memoir.
Garcia, Cristina.	*Dreaming in Cuban.* Knopf, 1992. The Aguero Sisters. Knopf, 1997.
Gibson, William.	*Count Zero.* Arbor House, 1986. *Mona Lisa Overdrive.* Bantam, 1988.
Godwin, Gail.	*The Good Husband.* Ballantine Books, 1994.
Goldberg, Myla.	*Bee Season.* Doubleday, 2000.
Goldman, William.	*Marathon Man.* Delacorte Press, 1974.
Gomez, Jewelle.	*The Gilda Stores.* Firebrand Books, 1991.
Gordon, Mary.	*The Shadow Man.* Random House, 1996. Memoir.
Hammett, Dashiell.	*Maltese Falcon.* Knopf, 1930.
Hellman, Lillian.	*Pentimento.* Little Brown, 1973. Memoir. *Maybe.* Little Brown, 1980. Memoir. *An Unfinished Woman.* Little Brown, 1969. Memoir
Hemingway Ernest.	*A Farewell to Arms.* Scribner, 1929. "The Short Sweet Life of Francis McComber." In *The Complete Short Stories of Ernest Hemingway.* Scribner, 1998.
Herlihy, James Leo.	*Midnight Cowboy.* Penguin, 1990.
Hijuelos, Oscar.	*The Mambo Kings Play Songs of Love.* Farrar, Strauss,1989.
Hinsey, Ellen.	*Cities of Memory.* Yale University Press, 1996.
Hoffman, Abbie.	*Soon to Be a Major Motion Picture.* Perigee, 1980. Memoir.
Hogan, Linda.	*Mean Spirit.* Atheneum, 1990.
Homer.	*The Odyssey.* Noonday Press, 1998. *Iliad.* Penguin, 1998.
Houston, Pam.	*Cowboys Are My Weakness.* W.W. Norton, 1992.

Jackson, Shirley.	"The Lotter*y*." Popular Library, 1949.
Jaffee, Annette Williams.	*Adult Education*. Leapfrog Press, 2000.
James, Henry.	*The Spoils of Poynton*. Dell, 1959.
Joyce, James.	*Portrait of the Artist as a Young Man*. Modern Library, 1916.
	The Trial. Modern Library, 1956.
	The Three Arched Bridge. Vintage International, 1998.
	The Liars Club. Viking, 1995. Memoir.
	The Beekeeper's Apprentice. St. Martins, 1994.
Kingsolver, Barbara.	*The Bean Trees*. Harper, 1998.
Kennedy, Pagan.	*The Exes*. Simon & Schuster, 1998.
Kinkaid, Jamaica.	*Annie John*. Farrar, Strauss, Giroux, 1985.
Kollontai, Alexandra.	*The Autobiography of a Sexually Emancipated Communist Woman*. Herder and Herder, 1975. Memoir.
LeCarre, John.	*Single & Single*. Scribner, 1999.
Leduc, Violette.	*la batarde*. Farrar, Straus, Giroux. 1965. Memoir.
Lee, Tanith.	*Lycanthia*. Daw, 1981.
LeGuin, Ursula.	*The Dispossessed*. Avon, 1974.
Lem, Stanislau.	*Solaris*. Walker, 1970.
Lessing, Doris.	*The Golden Notebook*. Simon & Shuster, 1960.
	Martha Quest. New American Library, 1964.
	A Proper Marriage. HarperCollins, 1964.
	A Ripple from the Storm. New American Library, 1966.
Lethem, Jonathon.	*As She Climbed Across the Table*. Doubleday, 1997.
	Amnesia Moon. Harcourt Brace,1996.
Levi, Primo.	*The Drowned and the Saved*. Simon & Schuster, 1988. Memoir.
	If Not Now, When? Penguin, 1985.
	The Reawakening. Collier Books, 1986. Memoir.
	The Periodic Table. (Stories.) Schocken Books, 1984.
London, Jack.	*To Build a Fire and Other Stories*. Bantam, 1990.
Matousek, Mark.	*Sex, Death, Enlightenment*. Riverhead Books, 1996.
McCourt, Frank.	*Angela's Ashes*. Touchstone, 1999. Memoir.
McInerney, Jay.	*Story of My Life*. Atlantic Monthly Press, 1988.
Melville, Herman.	*Moby Dick*. Macmillan, 1962.
Mailer, Norman.	*Armies of the Night*. New American Library, 1968.
Mitchell, Lauren Porosoff.	*Look at Me*. Leapfrog Press, 2000.
Morrison, Toni.	*Song of Solomon*. Knopf, 1977.
	Beloved. Knopf, 1987.
	Sula. Knopf, 1973.

Muhanji, Cherry.   *Her: A Novel.* Aunt Lute Books, 1991.
Muller, Karin.   *Hitchhiking Vietnam: A Woman's Solo Journey in an
         Elusive Land.* Globe Pequot Press, 1998. Memoir.
Murdoch, Iris.   *A Word Child.* Viking Press, 1975.
Nabokov, Vladimir.   *Lolita.* Putnam, 1980.
         Speak, Memory. Putnam, 1966. Memoir.
Neruda, Pablo.   *Memoirs.* Farrar, Straus & Giroux, 1976.
Oates, Joyce Carol.   *Blonde.* Harper Ecco, 1999.
O'Brien, Edna.   "Storm." (Story.) *Lantern Slides.*
         Farrar, Straus and Giroux, 1990.
Paley, Grace.   *Enormous Changes at the Last Minute.*
         Farrar, Straus and Giroux, 1974.
         Later the Same Day. Farrar, Straus and Giroux, 1985.
Piercy, Marge.   *Braided Lives.* Summit, 1981.
         City of Darkness, City of Light.
           Fawcett Columbine, 1996.
         Gone to Soldiers. Summit, 1987.
         He, She & It. Knopf, 1991.
         Sleeping with Cats. Morrow, 2002. Memoir.
         Small Changes. Doubleday, 1973.
         The Longings of Women. Fawcett Columbine, 1994.
         Three Women. Morrow, 1999.
         Woman on the Edge of Time. Knopf, 1976.
Piercy, Marge and
   Ira Wood.   *Storm Tide.* Ballantine, 1998.
Power, Susan.   *Grass Dancer.* Putnam, 1994.
Price, Richard.   *Clockers.* Houghton Mifflin, 1992.
Pynchon, Thomas.   *V.* Bantam Books, 1964.
         Vineland. Little, Brown & Co., 1990.
Quindlen, Anna.   *One True Thing.* Random House, 1994.
Rosenthal Richard.   *Rookie Cop.* Leapfrog Press, 2000. Memoir.
Roth, Philip.   *Portnoy's Complaint.* Random House, 1969.
         Sabbath's Theater. Houghton Mifflin, 1995.
Russ, Joanna.   *The Female Man.* Bantam Book, 1975.
Sarton, May.   *Encore.* W.W. Norton & Co., 1993. Memoir.
         (Any of Sarton's many memoirs are recommended.)
Scott, Melissa.   *Trouble and Her Friends.* TOR, 1994.
Shreve, Anita.   *The Weight of Water.* Little, Brown, 1997.
Slouka, Mark.   *Lost Lake.* Knopf, 1998.
Smith, Zadie.   *White Teeth.* Random House, 2000.
Sobell, Morton.   *On Doing Time.* Charles Scribner's Sons, 1974. Memoir.
Sophocles.   *Oedipus Rex.* Dover, 1993.

Sprigg, June.   *Simple Gifts: A Memoir of a Shaker Village.*
                           Knopf, 1998. Memoir.
Tangerlini, Arne.   *leo@fergusrules.com.* Leapfrog Press, 1999.
Thomas, Elizabeth
  Marshall.   *Reindeer Moon.* Pocket, 1991.
Thomas, Piri.   *Seven Long Times.* Arte Publico Press, 1994.
Thoreau, Henry.   *Walden.* Princeton University Press, 1989. Memoir.
Tolstoy, Leo.   *War & Peace.* Viking, 1982.
Traven, B.   *The Treasure of the Sierra Madre.* Hill & Wang, 1996.
Twain, Mark.   *A Connecticut Yankee in King Arthur's Court,*
                           Bantam, 1994.
                       Huckleberry Finn. Penguin, 1986.
Vidal, Gore.   *Palimpsest.* Random House, 1995. Memoir.
Vonnegut, Kurt.   *Slaughterhouse Five.* Delta, 1999.
Wallace, David
  Foster.   *Infinite Jest.* Little, Brown & Co., 1996.
Waugh, Evelyn.   *Brideshead Revisited.* Knopf, 1993.
Weldon, Fay.   *Darcy's Utopia.* Penguin Group, 1990.
Willis, Connie.   *To Say Nothing of the Dog.* Bantam, 1998.
Winterson, Jeanette.   *Oranges Are Not the Only Fruit.* Atlantic Monthly, 1987.
Wolfe, Virginia.   *Mrs. Dalloway.* Harcourt Brace & Co, 1925.
Wood, Ira.   *Going Public.* Zoland Books, 1991.
                       The Kitchen Man. Leapfrog Press, 1998.

X, Malcolm with
  Alex Haley.   *The Autobiography of Malcolm X.*
                           Grove Press, 1964. Memoir.
Yurick Sol.   *The Warriors.* Dell, 1979.
Zenophon.   *The Anabasis.* Harvard University Press, 1999.
Zinsser, William, ed. *Inventing the Truth: The Art and Craft of Memoir.*
                           Houghton Mifflin, 1987.

Also of use:

Jassin, Lloyd J. and Schecter, Steven C. *The Copyright Permission and Libel Handbook: A Step by Step Guide for Writers, Editors and Publishers.* Wiley, 1998.

Kirkpatrick, David D. "Report to the Authors Guild Midlist Books Study Committee." http://www.authorsguild.org/prmidlist.html

Resources

(UK resources have been independently researched by the UK publisher.)

UK

Writers' and Artists' Yearbook (A & C Black)
This is a comprehensive guide that is updated every year. Listed are publishers, agents, hundreds of magazines and newspapers, and poetry organizations in Britain and elsewhere in the world. It also contains a comprehensive directory of picture agencies and libraries and another of societies, associations and clubs.

The Writer's Handbook (Pan)
This annual handbook includes long alphabetical lists of UK and US magazines and newspapers, contact details for book publishers, relevant website addresses and festivals. It caters for article writers, novelists, playwrights, screen writers, and radio "scripters". It contains useful information for beginners and established writers.

The Society of Authors
84 Drayton Gardens
London SW10 9SD
Tel: 020 7373 6642
www.writers.org.uk

The Society of Authors is an independent trade union representing writers' interests in all aspects of the writing profession, including information about agents, publishers and others concerned with the book trade. In order to be a member you need to have had an item of work published.

Writers' News
PO Box 168
Wellington Street
Leeds
West Yorkshire LS1 1RF
Tel: 0113 238 8333
Fax: 0113 238 8330

A journal for writers featuring information and advice on all aspects of the world of writing, with market news on where to sell work, articles on various genres, and news about hundreds of writing competitions. Also published by the same group is *Writing Magazine*.

Little Magazines
www.little-magazines.org.uk

An online directory of little magazines published in the United Kingdom and Ireland that lists publishers of poetry, fiction and non-fiction and gives links to their websites.

International Directory of Little Magazines and Small Presses (Dustbooks)

This lists and updates almost 5,000 book and magazine publishers of poetry, fiction and non-fiction in every genre, and includes the names and addresses of editors and what they are looking for. See also *Literary Marketplace* and the useful line of books published by Writer's Digest Books, including *Poet's Market* and *Novel and Short Story Writers Market*.

Association of Authors' Agents

Dury House
34–43 Russell Street
London WC2B 5HA
Tel: 020 7344 1000
Fax: 020 7836 9541

The majority of established agencies in the UK belong to the Association. Although an agent who is not a member is not necessarily suspect, those who do belong have committed themselves to a high level of service and uphold a code of good practice.

US

Poets & Writers Inc.

www.pw.org

For writers submitting work to the US, this organization is a useful resource, particularly for the *Poets & Writers* magazine which lists writers conferences and workshops, new journals and material they are seeking, competitions to enter and anthologies seeking material. They also publish *A Directory of American Poets and Fiction Writers* which lists the names and addresses of writers and sometimes their agents as well.

Australia

The Australian Society of Authors

PO Box 1566
Strawberry Hills NSW 2012
Tel: (02) 9318 0877
Fax: (02) 9318 0530.
Email: office@asauthors.org
www.asauthors.org

The ASA protects authors and illustrators' rights and provides a contract advisory service, runs mentorships for new and emerging writers and offers advice about writing, copyright and publishing. You can join ASA even if you are not yet published.

NSW Writing Centre

PO Box 1056
Rozelle NSW 2039
Tel: (02) 9555 9757
Fax: (02) 9818 1327
Email: nswwc@ozemail.com.au
www.nswwriterscentre.org.au

The Centre offers literary resources and professional information to established and aspiring writers of all kinds, providing a venue for events and holding seminars and workshops in all genres.

South Africa

South African Writers' Network

www.futureshock.co.za

The SA Writers' Network offers resources for writers in numerous genres, including reference and research sources, online studying and publishing opportunities. Subscribers can also access more than 40 independent online/offline job markets and topical articles.

Index

Agents 146, 151–152
Allen, Woody 34
Allison, Dorothy 25, 68
Amis, Kingsley 91
Anabasis, The 68
Angela's Ashes 44–45
Atwood, Margaret 5, 95
autobiographical fiction 100

Baker, Russell 91–92
Ballard, J. G. 91–92
barriers to creativity 4, 129
Bastard Out of Carolina 25, 68
Bean Trees, The 42, 95
Bee Season 75, 95
Beginnings 13–29
Bogart, Humphrey 34
Bradley, Marion Zimmer 81
Brecht, Bertolt 85
Brideshead Revisited 70
Bronte, Charlotte 95
Burke James Lee 73
Burning Angel 73

Canterbury Tales, The 81
Casella, Casare 27
character driven fiction 74
Characterization 30–52, 67, 95, 101, 103
Characters (Naming) 36
characters drawn directly from life 32
Chaucer 81
chemistry involved in characters 30, 95
Clockers 34, 69

Columbo 34
computer database 115
Conan Doyle, Arthur 77

Conflicts 75–78
Conrad, Joseph 79, 97
Count Zero 27
Cowboys Are My Weakness 100

de Beauvoir, Simone 27
Description 105–114
Dialogue 53–64
Diary of a Tuscan Chef 27
Diary of Anne Frank, The 44, 97
Dinesen, Isaak 110
Direct versus Indirect Dialogue 62
Doctorow, E. L. 80, 95
Dos Passos, John 80

Electronic publishing 145–146, 157
Empire of the Sun 91
endings 82–83
Eve, Nomi 97

Fairy tales 67, 69
Family Orchard, The 97
Fisher, M. F. K. 93
Fitzgerald, F. Scott 97
Flanagan, Mary 27
formality versus informality in speech 56
Fowles, John 82, 97
French Lieutenant's Woman, The 82, 97
Friedman, Bruce Jay 31

Gibson, William 27
Goldberg, Myla 75, 96
Gordon, Mary 43
Great Gatsby, The 97

Hammet, Dashiell 27, 69
Harder They Come, The 57

Hellman, Lilian 26, 45, 91
Hemingway, Ernest 25, 54, 78, 96, 149
Herlihy, James Leo 74
Hijuelos, Oscar 26
Hitchcock, Alfred 69
Houston, Pam 100
Huckleberry Finn 42

idiomatic speech 54
Inciting Incident 69
Infinite Jest 157
International Directory of Little Magazines and Small Presses 176
Interviewing 117

Jackson, Shirley 79
Jaffee, Annette Williams 71
James, Henry 96, 116
Jane Eyre 95
jargon 46, 56, 117
Journaling 2, 87–88
Joyce, James 77, 149

Kafka, Franz 31, 35
Kingsolver, Barbara 42, 95
Kitchen Man, The 21, 38, 103, 109, 121, 123, 127, 152, 154, 159
Kumin, Maxine 71

Le Carré, John 69, 74
Lee, Tanith 16, 113
Lem, Stanislau 110
leo@fergusrules.com 112
Lessing, Doris 79, 95
Lolita 97
London, Jack 38
Look At Me 15, 101
Lord Jim 79
Lycanthia 16, 113

Maltese Falcon, The 69
Mambo Kings Play Songs of Love, The 26
marketing 142, 144, 149, 150, 155, 156, 158
Mason-Dixon 58
Matousek, Mark 91
McCourt, Frank 44

memoir 1–2, 5, 8–9, 10, 12–14, 24–29, 31, 36, 42–47, 54, 56, 63, 66, 75, 85–86, 88, 91, 110, 115–116, 119, 127, 140, 143
Memoirs of a Dutiful Daughter 27
Midnight Cowboy 74, 76
Minor characters 38, 46
Mitchell, Lauren Porosoff 15, 101
Moby Dick 78
Morris, Willie 93
Morrison, Toni 90, 156
Mrs. Dalloway 75
Multiple submissions 142, 154
multiple viewpoint 23, 82, 97–99

Nabokov, Vladimir 8, 97
narrator, omniscient 98

O'Brien, Edna 27
Odyssey, The 68
Olsen, Tillie 131
Out of Africa 110
over-plotting 66

Paley, Grace 42, 103
Palimpsest 26
plot 3, 12, 19, 22, 26, 32, 38, 63, 66–70, 73–74, 77–83, 89, 99, 103, 105, 107, 109, 149, 170
plot driven fiction 73, 74, 83
Poets & Writers 177
Portrait of the Artist as a Young Man 79
Practical information 140
Price, Richard 34, 69
Pritchett, V.S. 93
Publishers Marketing Association 149
Pynchon, Thomas 58

Quest, The 67, 69, 75
Questions to Ask of your Characters (Dossiers) 40

Ragtime 80, 95
Reading to Audiences 134, 138, 142
rejection letters 144, 148
Report to the Authors Guild Midlist Books Study Co 155, 157

Research 115–120
Rookie Cop 23–24, 57
Roth, Philip 31, 103, 125
Russ, Joanna 81

Sabbath's Theater 31
Samsa, Gregor 31
Sarton, May 90, 86, 87
Sayers, Dorothy 77
self hatred 31
sensory details 112
Seven Long Times 26, 90
Sex, Death, Enlightenment 91
Shadow Man, The 43
Shame 132
Sherlock Holmes 36, 77
Short Sweet Life of Francis McComber, The 25
Single & Single 69, 74
Solaris 110
Spoils of Poynton, The 116
Stern 31
Storm Tide 13, 54, 56, 69, 108
Surfacing 95

tags 37, 60, 63
Tangherlini, Arne 112

Thomas, Piri 26, 90
Three Penny Opera, The 83
transparent narrator 97
Traven, B. 81
Treasure of the Sierra Madre, The 81
Trial, The 35
Twain, Mark 42, 97

USA trilogy 80
Vanity Publishing 149, 157, 158
Victim, How Not to Write as a 43–45
Vidal, Gore 26, 90
Viewpoint 12, 14, 22, 23, 35, 39, 42, 81, 95–104, 114, 137
Vonnegut, Kurt 42

Wallace, David Foster 157
Wallace, Irving 54
Wanderers, The 68
Woolf, Virginia 75
work habits 6, 129–139
writers' groups 129, 134

Yurick, Sol 68, 95